THE

Less Waste No Fuss Kitchen

Simple steps to shop, cook and eat sustainably

Lindsay Miles

Hardie Grant

BOOKS

introduction

How do you go from being a supermarket-shopping, convenience-food-eating plastic addict who finds the idea of making things from scratch more than a little intimidating, to a mindful, seasonal(ish) eater who shops locally, eschews packaging (for the most part) and feels reasonably confident in the kitchen?

It doesn't happen overnight. But it can happen. Step by step, one switch at a time.

Your goal might not be a complete lifestyle makeover. But as you're here I'm guessing that you're interested in trying to reduce your impact – lowering your carbon footprint, avoiding excess packaging and minimising food waste. The most sustainable way to reduce your impact is in a way that works for you. I like to call it the 'no fuss' approach.

The kitchen, as you're about to find out, is a great place to start when it comes to reducing your impact. There are so many things that are no longer sustainable with our current food system, but also so many opportunities to tweak our habits and make better buying decisions. Plus, everybody eats!

First, though, let's get one thing clear: there is no such thing as 'planetarily perfect'. The closest thing that comes to my mind is somebody working the land, growing all their own food, saving all their seeds, preserving their entire harvest, capturing sun and wind energy, and composting everything (and no, I don't mean *only* the food scraps).

Do you know anyone who lives like this?

I didn't think so. Me neither.

This lifestyle just isn't realistic or practical (or desirable!) for the majority of us. And anything outside of it has some kind of footprint. So we're going to drop this notion of 'perfect' altogether, and go for doing what we can.

Other people will have different priorities, and make different choices to us. That's not to say these are 'better' or 'worse'; they are simply different choices for different circumstances.

Too often when we read about reducing our footprint, we come across 'should' and 'should not' statements. Not in this book. Its purpose is to give you the ideas and tools to make changes and feel positive about the things you can do, not guilty about those things you can't. And anyway, no one does all of the things, all of the time.

Instead, I want to help you understand the issues so you can choose what you want to do. I'm here to help you navigate the complex and sometimes conflicting options when it comes to eating ethically and sustainably, support you in reducing your waste and lowering your footprint in a way that fits in with your lifestyle, and persuade you that spending a bit more time in the kitchen can be as fun (and delicious) as it is rewarding!

Planetarily perfect might not be a thing, but there is plenty of opportunity to have a positive impact through the food we buy, how we buy it, and what we do with it once we get it home. And when I say plenty, I mean every single day.

Our modern-day food system (and why it's no longer sustainable)

It's hard to imagine a time without supermarkets, but it was on 4 August 1930 that the first true supermarket opened: King Kullen, in the United States, operating under the slogan 'Pile it high. Sell it cheap'. Prior to this, shoppers made separate trips to the greengrocer, butcher, fishmonger, dry goods store, general store and bakery, where shop assistants would fetch, measure out and pack everything the customer required.

These new supermarkets had food departments and self-service, and by opening multiple outlets (the beginning of supermarket chains) they were able to sell larger volumes of food, lowering the prices. The idea spread to other parts of the world: the first UK supermarket opened in 1951 and the first Australian supermarket opened in 1960.

Today, 84 per cent of US shoppers buy their food primarily at a supermarket or supercentre (a discount department store that also sells a full range of groceries). In the UK less than 2 per cent of shoppers buy groceries from independent stores. The two biggest Australian supermarkets, Coles and Woolworths, along with Aldi make up 73 per cent of the Australian grocery market.

Supermarkets offer us food that is cheap, uniform in size and appearance, blemish-free, clean and pre-packaged, some ready-to-eat, abundant no matter what the season and from all the corners of the globe.

But this isn't actually how food grows. There are systems in place that allow this endless array of perfect produce, and these systems have limitations that are putting increasing strain on our planet.

The choice we are offered in supermarkets is eye-opening.

It seems that no matter where our supermarket is located, we can buy salmon from Alaska, apple juice from the UK, asparagus from Peru, white wine from California, olive oil from Italy, butter from New Zealand and biscuits from Australia.

The average supermarket today stocks 40,000–50,000 different product lines. The problem with this 'choice' is that all of these products have to be shipped, flown and/or freighted over hundreds (or thousands) of kilometres from farms and factories to the stores. Take imported asparagus, for example. In 2014 Australians spent almost $20 million on asparagus imported from countries including Peru and Mexico – covering distances of more than 15,000 kilometres (9400 miles). The USA imported 228,000 tonnes (502.4 million pounds) of asparagus from Mexico, Peru and Chile in 2017. And that's just the asparagus.

The distances over which food items are transported during their journey from producer to shopper are known as 'food miles'.

This means trucks on the roads, planes in the sky and container ships on the ocean, burning fuel and releasing emissions into the atmosphere. Transportation of food accounts for around 11 per cent of the greenhouse gases that an average household in the USA or the UK generates annually as a result of food consumption.

Trade is nothing new. Camels were domesticated in 3000 BCE, which allowed the opening of trade routes to import spices and other products. Later, boats expanded trade further. But trade today has been completely transformed: not just the types of products or the way they are shipped, but also the scale.

Products with a longer shelf life (or those that can be transported frozen) will often be shipped by boat or transported by truck rather than flown by plane, which reduces overall transport emissions. But this is not the case with many imported fresh fruits and vegetables. Fresh produce has a very short shelf life and needs to be air-freighted to reach stores soon after picking. Some very quick-to-perish foods such as berries may even be flown to stores within their country of origin.

Food miles aren't the biggest greenhouse gas contributor when it comes to food production and consumption, but they are still significant when we consider that much of this transportation is so that we, as shoppers, have a 'choice' of products.

This 'choice' often doesn't even mean exotic ingredients. In many cases supermarkets are sourcing products from far-flung places when they could find something local that is equally as good. It's not that it's necessarily cheaper or better to do so – sometimes there's the prestige associated with stocking certain products, or it's the power that big corporations have to push their own brands into stores.

Other times, the supermarkets wish to sell items that are not available locally at certain times of the year. This is particularly true of fresh food.

Walk into any supermarket at any time of year and you'll see a similarly abundant, colourful display of fresh food.

A quick look at the 'country of origin' labels (which are required by law to be displayed on all fresh produce in Australia, the UK, the USA and many other countries) reveals much of this produce is not grown locally, and may have journeyed hundreds if not thousands of (food) miles to reach the store.

This is because plants need specific conditions to grow. The majority of fruit trees produce a harvest just once a year.

Some crops keep well; others can't be stored for long. Some plants love the cold while others need a tropical climate to bear fruit. Some need dry conditions; some require high rainfall; others may require a particular soil type or only grow at altitude.

Back in the 1930s, before the first supermarkets arrived and the globalisation of our food system began, shoppers had to make do with whatever produce was in season or stored well, along with occasional imports. Now we expect to head to the store and find every ingredient we can imagine, no matter the time of year.

Remember that imported asparagus? Asparagus is typically harvested for a period of three to six weeks in spring. By taking advantage of regional diversity (with warmer areas producing first, and colder areas producing later) and different varieties (producing asparagus spears earlier or later in the season), it may be possible for a store to stock local asparagus for two to three months of the year. But what about those other nine months? The stores can decide to sell only local asparagus when it is in season, and offer other delicious seasonal vegetables for the other months of the year. Or, they can import asparagus for those nine out-of-season months.

Almost always, supermarkets choose to do the latter.

Huge amounts of produce are being exported for part of the year and imported for the rest of the year, generating significant emissions, all so that we can all purchase out-of-season vegetables all year round.

When it comes to fruit and vegetables, what appears to be an excellent selection is only a fraction of the varieties grown.

Because supermarkets are big, we tend to think they offer us an enormous amount of choice. But the reality is that most of the products on offer are processed food products.

There are over 750 varieties of eating apple grown throughout the world. We're familiar with Braeburn, Royal Gala, Granny Smith, Jazz, Golden (and Red) Delicious, Pink Lady ... but that's only 1 per cent of the varieties being grown.

With other types of produce the choice is even more limited. There are at least 300 types of edible banana grown in the world, yet just one variety dominates the supermarket shelves: the Cavendish banana.

Carrots can be purple, white, red and yellow as well as the more usual orange colour, but you'd never know that looking at most supermarket produce sections.

The reasons behind these limited choices has less to do with taste, health or nutrition, and more to do with profit. Supermarkets prioritise the varieties that are the most pest-resistant (because these are easier to grow and more profitable), fastest growing and highest yielding (meaning farmers can produce more crops with their land each year), that ripen more slowly and bruise less easily (meaning they can be harvested mechanically, are easier to transport long distances, and appear 'fresher' for longer in stores), among other considerations.

'Pile it high. Sell it cheap.'

This means that millions of us are missing out on all kinds of tasty, locally grown and nutritious produce that never makes it to the supermarket, and so much of the joy that eating delicious and fresh food brings.

Over the years, supermarkets have conditioned us to expect fruit and vegetables that are uniform in appearance.

Supermarket produce is usually blemish-free: without unusual colouring, darkened skin, lumps, bumps and other minor marks, or the small holes created by caterpillars and other insects (particularly in leafy greens). None of these affect taste.

We sometimes forget that fruit and vegetables are mostly grown outside, exposed to the elements, and that in nature, appearance varies and may be 'imperfect'. There are natural ways to control pests, including maintaining hedgerows that provide a habitat for predators, rotating the crops grown in a field over a few years (because particular pests love particular plants), companion planting and planting smaller fields, so that if a crop does get attacked by pests, they are less likely to spread.

But these methods don't lend themselves to automated processes such as mechanical harvesting, or to big yields. And so, many farmers who don't want their crops to be rejected by supermarkets, and who want to ensure harvests that return the investment they put in, turn to pesticides.

Pesticides are chemical substances used to prevent, destroy, repel or reduce pests, including insects (insecticides), weeds (herbicides) and microorganisms (bactericides or fungicides). Around 2.5 million tonnes (5.6 billion pounds) of pesticides are used worldwide every year, with over 450,000 tonnes (1 billion pounds) used in the United States alone.

The safety of many of these chemicals often comes into question, and it has been estimated that 25 million agricultural workers worldwide experience unintentional pesticide poisonings each year.

Due to health concerns many pesticides have now been banned – but bans are not always global, and a pesticide might be banned in one country but freely available for use in another. For example, the pesticide Paraquat, which has been linked to Parkinson's disease, has been banned in thirty-two countries (including China and countries in Europe) but not in the USA or Australia. Organophosphates, a group of pesticides linked to lymphoma, leukaemia and childhood cancers, have been banned in the USA, and their use is restricted in Europe, but they continue to be widely used in Australia.

It makes sense to question the effectiveness of local bans when trade is global – especially when we remember that much of our fresh produce is imported from overseas for part of the year.

Our industrialised global food system is also responsible for vast amounts of food being wasted every day.

Supermarkets do not want to sell fresh produce that is scarred, dented or nibbled. But their obsession with appearance goes way beyond blemishes.

Anything that does not meet the supermarket's definition of what a product 'should' look like simply does not make it to the shelves. And so, bananas that are deemed too fat, too thin, too straight or too curved are rejected, along with oranges that are too squat or elongated, sweetcorn that's too short, asparagus that's too wide or bendy … and so the list goes on.

An estimated 20–40 per cent of fruit and vegetables are rejected before they reach the supermarket simply because they do not meet cosmetic standards.

Supermarkets also encourage shoppers to waste food. Whether by pre-packing produce into plastic with a cheaper price than the loose equivalent, through buy-one-get-one-free or three-for-the-price-of-two offers, or by strategically placing those essentials we're after at the back of the store so that we have to walk past all the tempting snack foods and special deals we don't actually need to get to them, supermarkets are masters of encouraging us to buy more than we need.

Then there are the 'best before' dates printed on the packaging. These are simply guidelines to advise us when something is at its best, but are often misconstrued as the date when things are no longer safe to eat. Plenty of food that is still perfectly edible is binned simply because it has exceeded a 'best before' date.

We, the food shoppers, play our own part in wasting food.

Through overbuying, incorrect storage, lack of cooking skills, forgetfulness and changes of plans, we often fail to eat the food we buy. Around 40 per cent of everything the average householder throws away is food waste. Some of that is pips, cores, skins, rinds and inedible bits, but the majority is food that could have been eaten.

From farm to plate, when all of this is added together, globally it's estimated that one third of all food produced for human consumption never gets eaten.

That's not just a waste of food; that's a waste of all of the resources that were used in the growing, harvesting, processing and transporting of this food – including nutrients, carbon, water, land, energy, labour and time. The footprint of food waste is huge.

In fact, in 2013 the United Nations declared that if food waste was a country, it would be the third biggest emitting country in the world, behind China and the USA.

Plastic and packaging are becoming a problem.

Packaging is used for hygiene reasons, to maintain freshness and to provide protection and reduce damage when goods are transported. It also gives companies an opportunity to brand their products and make them attractive to customers, and to incentivise us to buy more by creating larger pack sizes.

It's easy to see the particular appeal of plastic from the point of view of stores and manufacturers: it is lightweight and so requires less fuel to transport (which reduces carbon emissions). Plastic is strong, waterproof and more resistant to damage, especially compared to paper and cardboard, and can be transparent and colourless, meaning the items inside can be easily seen by the shopper. (Glass is also transparent, but heavier to transport and much more breakable.)

But this plastic is choking our landfills and our oceans, harming wildlife by suffocation, entanglement and ingestion. Once in the environment it doesn't break down; instead it breaks up into microplastics: tiny pieces of plastic that have been detected in the water, soil, air and the food we eat.

Not to mention that over 99 per cent of plastic is made from petrochemicals (fossil fuels like oil and natural gas). Plastic production is responsible for around 6 per cent of global oil consumption, the same proportion as the global aviation sector.

In 2018, *The Guardian* estimated that British supermarkets alone create more than 800,000 tonnes (1.8 billion pounds) of plastic packaging waste each year.

We may hope that our plastic packaging will be recycled, yet this is not as straightforward as we like to think.

Plastics need to be recycled by type, which can be challenging, particularly when they are fused together in packaging. Plastic packaging is also easily contaminated by food, making it harder to recycle. Many plastics are damaged by air and heat during reprocessing, meaning they are not recycled back into packaging but are downgraded into other products.

For recycling systems to work, there has to be demand for recycled products. New plastic is cheap and there is currently little incentive for manufacturers to choose material with recycled content.

And that's assuming recycling is a possibility. It's easy for a manufacturer to print 'please recycle' on the label, but if there is no recycling system for that particular material where we live, it will not be recycled, even if we put it in the recycling bin.

In 2018 *National Geographic* estimated that only 9 per cent of all the plastic ever made has likely been recycled. It's a sobering thought, considering that 406 million tonnes (896 billion pounds) of plastic is produced worldwide every year, of which more than a third is used for packaging.

Almost all of our packaging, plastic or not, is single-use and uses precious resources. Aluminium and steel cans are made from metals mined from the ground, paper and cardboard are made from trees that have to be chopped down, and bioplastic is made from plants such as corn and sugar cane that still require water and nutrients to grow on land that could be used to produce edible crops.

On a planet where resources are increasingly strained, we need to shift to using less packaging, not more.

This is just a snapshot of some of the dilemmas our global food system faces.

There are whole books, often multiple books, dedicated to each of these problems, exploring them in more detail than I have. But I'm not interested in dwelling on the problems. I'm interested in the solutions.

With a global food system as complex as ours, there's no one clear, perfect solution to changing the way we shop, cook and eat. This isn't about labelling supermarkets as the bad guys. They have made food both more affordable and more accessible to millions of people. But today we recognise that rising carbon emissions, the use of chemicals, excessive packaging and food waste are putting increasing strain on our planet and do not add up to a sustainable way to do business. No doubt supermarkets and other big businesses will have an important role to play in our new sustainable food system. But when companies are big, change can be slow.

We don't need to wait for them. It's time to do things differently.

We eat at least three times a day, every day – which means plenty of opportunity to make simple switches.

The rest of this book is dedicated to exploring all the ways that you can make a difference through the way you choose, store and use your food, and giving you the tools and confidence to make changes that contribute to a more sustainable way of eating.

The most important thing is that we feel informed about the issues, connected with our food choices and empowered to take action. We can be more knowledgeable and confident about the ingredients we buy, what we put in the recycling bin, and how to keep our landfill waste low.

This may mean we continue to shop at supermarkets, and tweak what we buy. It may mean that we explore the other options locally, and decide to branch out to other places to supplement the regular supermarket shop. And it may mean that we wave the supermarket goodbye completely. It definitely doesn't mean we have to take the fun out of eating!

We all feel differently about different issues and have different capacities to make change. We can use our own moral compass, along with the solutions that are most accessible and realistic for us, to do the best we can.

Rather than seeing this book as an instruction manual, see it as a buffet of ideas. Choose the ideas that resonate with you, the ones you know can fit in with your life, the ones that get you excited. We're not going for perfection. We're going for better. That's within the grasp of all of us.

before we begin

Something to remember throughout this book is the idea of focusing on doing what you can. Too much energy is spent feeling guilty about things we cannot control, and it will be better spent feeling good about the things that we can change.

Just because a particular choice might be deemed super sustainable (by a group of scientists with complex sets of data and clever algorithms, or by somebody you've never met on social media) it doesn't mean making that choice works for everyone. It might not work for us. And that's okay – there are so many ways we can do better. Sustainability isn't just about the planet: it has to be sustainable for us, too.

Change looks different for everyone. And no one (absolutely no one) is perfect. Nor do we live in an ideal world where ethical options are always available in the way we'd like them to be and at a price we can afford. In this ideal world we'd have all the time we needed, the skills to cook and store everything we purchased correctly and the energy to do it – but for most of us, reality differs!

With every decision, we have to consider what will be realistic and practical for us.

Accessibility

No two cities are the same. Some parts of the world don't support year-round agriculture and some only support certain types of food growing and farming. City dwellers have very different options to people living in smaller country towns or those in remote and rural areas. This includes the types of shops, the types of food available and access to allotments or community gardens.

Budget

Our bank balances sometimes dictate the choices we make, however much we believe in the alternatives. A single-income household with lots of mouths to feed is in a different situation to a double-income household with no children. Generally, more disposable income means more flexibility and freedom of choice.

Spare time and energy levels

Not everyone has time to make everything from scratch; not everyone sees cooking as a fun way to be creative or relax. Physically demanding jobs, long working hours, looking after families, emotional challenges and all kinds of other factors play into what we're capable of doing.

Food intolerances, allergies and dietary needs

Not everyone can tolerate gluten, or grains, or dairy. Not everyone thrives on a vegan diet. Allergies can be a real concern for some of us. Best for the planet doesn't always mean what's best for our wellbeing.

Taste

Our tastebuds operate completely independently of any talk of carbon emissions or unnecessary packaging. As adults, we can reason with ourselves and make sacrifices, but we also get to make exceptions for the things we truly don't want to go without. With kids, reasoning may be harder. Plus, if you want a balanced diet for your child, and the only vegetable they'll eat is imported asparagus, then you're going to be making decisions based on their health as much as any planetary ideals.

Values

Different issues motivate us differently. What's 'best' for the planet isn't necessarily aligned with what our values tell us is the right thing to do. If we don't want to compromise our personal beliefs, we don't need to. There are plenty of ways to make positive choices.

Capacity for change

Change can often mean unlearning what we've done for years, and relearning a whole new way of doing things. For some, change is exciting and something to be embraced. For others it's less easy, especially when we've been doing things the old way for a long time. For every person who decides to completely overhaul their life, there's someone who starts with a single swap. There is no shame in starting small.

It is important to remember that change doesn't happen overnight, nor does it happen in a straight line. It takes time to research new things, learn the locations of markets or layouts of different stores, adjust schedules, tweak budgets and form new habits. Take on just enough to keep it manageable for you. If you find an idea that you like the sound of, give it a go. When there's something that doesn't appeal to you or you know won't work for you, don't get angry or feel guilty. Just move on to the next thing. It's common when you change your habits for things to take a bit longer. You could probably walk into your regular grocery store right now and do your entire weekly shop with your eyes closed. Shaking things up is going to slow things down – at first. Soon enough you'll settle into it and figure out a routine that works for you. In the meantime, if it starts to feel a little overwhelming or unmanageable, just ... slow ... down. The opportunity to change and do better is always there, and it will wait until you're ready.

the three pillars

This book will focus on three key, interconnected ways we can make changes.

Plastic and packaging

Our waste footprint (the plastic and packaging we use) is easy to see because we are the ones selecting it from the store shelves, and we are the ones who put it in the bin. A significant proportion of the plastic packaging we buy is not recycled, but we can try to choose recyclable packaging wherever possible and ensure we are recycling it correctly; we can try to avoid the most overpackaged products, or we can look for ways to do without packaging altogether.

Carbon footprint and climate change

Our carbon footprint is the amount of greenhouse gases released as a result of our activities and choices. Greenhouse gases are those that trap heat in the earth's atmosphere, and rising emissions of these gases are clearly linked to global warming and climate change. Every single thing we do has an impact (even our breathing releases carbon dioxide into the atmosphere!) but we can definitely make choices to lessen our impact through what we eat.

Food waste and landfill

While food waste occurs at every step in the growing and production process, once we make the choice to buy something and bring it home, it is up to us not to let it go to waste. More than a third of what we throw away is food. Whether we're ensuring edible food doesn't go bad, or composting to ensure inedible food isn't landfilled or incinerated, reducing food waste is within our grasp.

How is plastic and packaging linked to my carbon footprint?

Conventional plastic is made from fossil fuels, but because it is lightweight and uses less fossil fuels to transport, it actually has a lower carbon footprint than other packaging types such as glass, cardboard and metal, especially if these are shipped from overseas. To reduce our plastic but also keep our carbon footprint down, we need to prioritise products with less or no packaging and opt for locally produced food.

How is my carbon footprint linked to food waste and landfill?

Food waste that ends up in landfill generates methane, a potent greenhouse gas. While composting eliminates any methane emissions, it's important to reduce the edible food going to waste. That food was planted, fertilised, watered, harvested, packed and transported before it reached our shopping basket, and each of those steps used energy and resources. Eating the food we produce is a much better use of resources than letting it end up in the bin, even when it's a compost bin!

How is food waste and landfill linked to plastic and packaging?

Because most of the plastic packaging we buy is not recycled, reducing our consumption directly reduces what we send to landfill. However, plastic packaging can both cause and reduce food waste. On the one hand, we may buy more than we need when food is pre-packaged; on the other, plastic packaging can extend the life of our food, particularly fresh produce. To avoid creating more waste when we reduce our packaging, we need to store things to make them last, and get better at using them up.

how to use this book

In the next three parts we will look at each of our three pillars to see how we can change our food shopping and storage habits to make a difference. Then we'll finish up in the kitchen, where we'll explore more ways to put these ideas into action when we cook and eat.

Rather than read this book from start to finish, you may prefer to jump straight to the bits that interest you most. The guide on the next few pages outlines some of the practical actions we'll be looking at. Think of it a little like a menu: choose your favourites or the ones that resonate most. You don't have to go for everything ... but you can! To get started, consider which issues you feel most strongly about and how much time and energy you're willing to invest in them. This will help you decide what to explore first.

There's an ancient Japanese proverb that says 'vision without action is a daydream'. There is no change without action, so less dreaming, and more doing. Whether you're prioritising one issue above all else, or caring about a number of different things and trying to improve a little bit in each of these areas, changing for the better is always going to be, well, better!

choose what you'll do about:
plastic and packaging

Start here Fuss level +	**Next steps** Fuss level ++	**Next level** Fuss level +++
Make it a habit to always remember reusable shopping bags when going to the store.	Switch to reusable produce bags when buying fruit and vegetables.	Swap out plastic food wrap in the kitchen (turn to page 126 for some alternatives).
Choose more unpackaged fruit and vegetables at the store.	Choose unpackaged bread and grocery cupboard ingredients at the store.	Ask for deli and food service counter items to be placed in your own containers, or wrapped in paper (turn to page 55 for tips on how to approach this).
Prioritise recyclable packaging when buying groceries (turn to page 37 for help with your recycling options).	Choose non-plastic (recyclable) alternatives for pre-packaged grocery items.	Buy groceries unpackaged.
Buy some produce at the local farmers' market.	Subscribe to a vegetable box delivery scheme (turn to page 64 to find out how these work).	Sign up to a CSA (community supported agriculture) share for a season.
Take a stand: pick one grocery item that only comes packaged in plastic to stop buying altogether.	Reduce how often you buy products that only come packaged in plastic.	Make some grocery items that are hard to find without plastic packaging from scratch (turn to page 189 for an easy cracker recipe).

choose what you'll do about:
carbon footprint and climate change

Start here Fuss level +	**Next steps** Fuss level ++	**Next level** Fuss level +++
Look for locally grown fruit and vegetables (page 67 has options for finding food grown in your area).	Choose more locally grown and produced chilled and frozen products.	Buy locally grown and produced dry goods and bulk foods.
Reduce the amount of meat per portion, and/or try one day a week meat-free (turn to page 174 for some new ideas on how to cook vegetables).	Replace red meat (which has a higher carbon footprint) with poultry.	Go vegetarian (meat-free) for meals prepared or eaten at home.
For breakfast, swap dairy milk for locally made (or homemade) plant milk (e.g. oat, almond, rice; turn to page 183 for an easy plant milk recipe).	Choose locally produced, softer cheeses for lunches and snacks – or swap cheese for hummus.	For dinner, switch animal proteins (meat, seafood, dairy) to plant proteins (e.g. pulses, nuts and seeds).
Buy some organic fruit and vegetables.	Prioritise organic grains and cereal products (turn to page 96 to learn which cereals are most reliant on chemical fertilisers).	Swap to a wholly organic diet.
Choose products with certified sustainable palm oil rather than non-certified palm oil.	Reduce the number of products purchased that contain palm oil (turn to page 97 to find out what all the fuss is about palm oil).	Stop buying products that contain palm oil.

choose what you'll do about:
food waste and landfill

Start here
Fuss level +

Next steps
Fuss level ++

Next level
Fuss level +++

Start here — Fuss level +	Next steps — Fuss level ++	Next level — Fuss level +++
Find a place to take your food scraps for composting rather than putting them in the general waste bin.	Set up a compost bin to process your food scraps (turn to page 134 to discover which system might be right for you).	Add your compost bin to *sharewaste.com* to encourage the neighbours to compost too.
Keep a food waste diary to find out what you're throwing away (turn to page 33 to learn how to keep a food waste diary).	Learn how to store fruit and vegetables correctly to extend their life.	Learn how to use skins, leaves, stalks and crusts in meals.
Check your pantry and fridge before going grocery shopping to avoid buying things you already have.	Write a shopping list to avoid impulse purchases and buying more than is needed (turn to page 107 to remind yourself why people waste food).	Plan meals a few days in advance to avoid buying too much and ensure things get used before they go bad.
Set up an 'eat me first' tray or shelf in the fridge so everybody knows what needs using up.	Use the freezer to extend the life of food that won't get eaten within a few days.	Try out one food preservation technique (dehydrating, fermenting, pickling or canning; turn to page 204 to learn about preservation techniques).
Learn what 'best before' and 'use by' dates mean to avoid throwing edible food in the bin (turn to page 108 for a simple guide).	Label jars and storage containers with names and dates to help rotate food and use it up more quickly.	Love your leftovers: eat them for lunch or make a plan to incorporate them in the next meal rather than binning them.

knowing our habits

If we're going to reduce our carbon footprint, use less packaging and limit our food waste, we're going to have to change some of the things we buy, as well as how and where we buy them, and we're going to spend a little bit more time in the kitchen.

Some of the things. A little bit more time.

One of the biggest mistakes I made before the start of my less waste journey was putting off taking action for 'later' – the hypothetical stage of my life when I could afford to buy a big block of land and grow my own vegetables and buy everything else organic, and when I had more time to make food from scratch. Worse, I was guilty of waiting for others to take action so that I did not have to.

What I realised was, 'later' might never come, and waiting for others is frustrating; change from them never comes as fast as we'd like. We don't need to wait – we can take action right away. Doing something feels good.

The following exercises encourage you to take stock of your current life situation: how much you have to spend on food, how much food you're currently wasting, what packaging you could be recycling, and your supermarket shopping habits. These are great first steps in figuring out how and where you can make effective changes at your own pace.

how to: work out your grocery budget

If our goal is to buy the best food we can at a price we can afford, we need to know what we can actually afford. It's a good idea to first figure out how much we currently spend on our weekly food shop (including takeaway and eating out). And I don't mean how much we *allocate* for spending on groceries, or what we *think* we spend – because these are often very different things! Wishful thinking is not going to help; we need facts.

Understanding how we spend can help us identify priorities for change. Knowing what our grocery budget is can help stop us comparing every swap on a cost basis with its non-organic or plastic-wrapped or imported equivalents; it can help us look at the bigger picture of our overall spend, and make better buying decisions.

Figuring out what we spend on food might seem painful, but it won't take long, and it will be worth it. All you need is your bank and credit card statements for a month, a pen and paper.

Go through your statements for the month and wherever you notice you spent money on food, highlight it. (If you sometimes pay for food with cash, you'll need to look at your cash withdrawals and ensure you're including this too.) Don't leave anything out, even if you feel like it was an exception or one-off – these things pop up more often than we think, and we want to be as accurate as possible. Break it down into categories: grocery shopping, takeaway beverages, snacks when out and about, meals at cafes and restaurants, alcohol, or whatever makes sense for you.

If you want to be really thorough, you can also go through your grocery store receipts. These are going to tell you exactly what you spend on different categories (such as bread, vegetables and snacks). If you don't normally keep your grocery store receipts, make an effort to keep them for the next week. Yes, till receipts are usually paper and many of us prefer to go paperless where we can, but it is going to help us reduce our waste down the track.

We might notice that loose broccoli costs more than pre-packaged broccoli, or that milk in glass is more expensive than milk in plastic. But if we also see that we're now spending less on bread and other vegetables, for example, and we are within our grocery budget, we will feel more at ease.

As you start to change the things you buy, the amounts you spend on different things will probably change too. It's a good idea to keep receipts while you find your way. Not only can you keep track of your overall spend, but if you notice that one category is going wildly over budget you can look for other categories to borrow from, or think about ways to rein it back in.

how to: keep a food waste diary

Food gets wasted at every step of the journey from field to plate. Some of this is outside our control – but once we buy food and bring it home, it is up to us to try not to waste it. It's taken a lot of effort to grow it, get it from farm to store and into our homes, and that includes the time and money it took us to go to the shops and buy it. Just putting it straight in the bin uneaten is a waste on every level!

We might waste food due to:

+ Forgetfulness
+ Changing plans
+ Portion sizes that are bigger than we can eat
+ Buying too much
+ Best-before and use-by dates passing
+ Disliking the taste, appearance or texture
+ Incorrect storage
+ Not knowing how to cook it properly

The food we throw away can be divided into three categories: the still edible, the truly inedible (including the food we don't *think* is edible and so discard), and the once-edible food that has spoiled and goes uneaten.

Because there's often a big gap between what we think we waste and what we actually waste, the first thing to do is find out what food we throw away, and why. From this we can look at our habits and make changes. For example, if we are constantly throwing away bananas, maybe we need to buy fewer bananas, or start looking for ways to use up the excess. If we are constantly throwing away food on Saturdays and we do a weekly shop on Monday, maybe we're just buying too much and can think about doing a smaller shop, and topping up later in the week.

First, choose your timeframe. Longer is better – a week is good, a fortnight is great and a month is marvellous! Each day, record the food (edible, inedible and spoiled) that you threw away, the time (or which meal it was closest to) and the quantity or amount. Depending on what it is, you can weigh it, count it, or guesstimate – you'll probably find a mix works best.

Finally, think about why you're throwing it away. Try to be as specific as possible and drill down not just to a general 'why' but a more specific 'really why'. For example, 'I didn't like the taste' could be refined to 'it contained too much spinach' or 'it was way too salty'; 'I didn't feel like eating the leftovers' might actually mean 'I've eaten these leftovers for five days straight and I was sick of them' or 'I had a hard day and fancied pizza instead'.

If you didn't throw away anything in a particular day, it's worth noting why for that too. Was it that you were amazingly organised and diligent, or was it that you ate out or had leftovers? Remember, we're not just trying to understand what food we waste but also our habits.

Ask yourself:

+ What foods did I throw away most?
+ What were my most common reasons for wasting food?
+ Were there any surprises?

It's worth continuing to keep track of food waste as we start to make changes to the things we buy. There's no point spending more on fresh produce if it just ends up in the compost, and packaging-free groceries that never get cooked are ultimately wasting more than the packaging that was avoided.

how to: create a recycling checklist

In an ideal world we'd be able to buy everything without packaging. The reality is that most of us will have to compromise somewhere along the line and will need to buy some things in packaging at least some of the time. So which packaging is best?

Before we can make these choices, we need to know what packaging can be recycled in our area. Theoretically recyclable does not mean *actually recycled where we live*. Printing 'please recycle' on a packet doesn't make something magically recyclable. If the infrastructure doesn't exist to process that material, it won't get recycled, even if you put it in your recycling bin.

Make a list of the kinds of packaging materials you purchase and find out how you could be recycling it.

Most packaging will tell you what it's made of. With plastics there's usually a number inside a chasing arrow symbol that translates to a specific type of plastic; alternatively, you'll see the abbreviated letters. For example, plastic number 1 might also appear as PET or PETE, plastic number 4 as LDPE and so on. A magnet will tell you if a metal is steel (it's magnetic) or aluminium (it's not magnetic). To help you get started, I've included a quick guide to common packaging materials on page 37.

Your local council will be able to tell you what is and isn't recyclable. Some councils have helpful websites detailing exactly what can be recycled in kerbside bin collections and at other locations in the area. If in doubt, call and ask to speak to the waste officer or sustainability officer. Most councils contract their recycling out to an external company, so you may be advised to check with the recycler directly, which you can do via their website or by phone.

Recycling contracts are often short term (they rely on markets dictated by supply and demand) so it's worth checking in with your local council every six months to see if anything has changed.

As well as checking with your local council, find out if TerraCycle (a private company that specialises in recycling hard-to-recycle plastics) operate in your area, what materials they accept for recycling and how you can recycle them (usually by mail or at specified drop-off locations).

Once you know which packaging types can be easily recycled and which ones cannot, it's going to inform your future choices. All things being equal, it's better to choose the packaging that is recyclable over the one that is not.

Steel	Canned food including fruit, vegetables, beans and fish products
Aluminium	Drinks cans including soft drinks, mixers and beer, and foil
Glass	Jars and bottles including condiments, sauces and oils
Cardboard and paper	Often used for bakery products and some grains
Paperboard	A mix of paper and plastic used for chilled milk cartons
UHT/Tetra Pak	A mix of paper, plastic and aluminium used for long-life liquids
Laminated foil	Used in stand-up pouches for liquids, cat food and packaged coffee beans: looks like metal but feels like plastic
Metallised film	Metallic plastic used for snack foods such as potato chip packets
Plastic #1 PET	Clear and colourless packaging including drinks bottles
Plastic #2 HDPE	Opaque plastic milk containers
Plastic #3 PVC	Some clingfilm or clingwrap
Plastic #4 LDPE	Plastic bags, bread bags, six-pack rings, some food containers
Plastic #5 PP	Sauce bottles, yoghurt and margarine tubs
Plastic #6 Polystyrene PS	Expanded polystyrene used in 'foam' food containers and meat trays; non-expanded polystyrene used for bread tags
Plastic #7 'other'	Includes bioplastic and compostable plastic

how to: assess your supermarket shop

When I first made a commitment to reduce my waste, I actually started out not by tracking down a specialist store or locating a farmers' market but by going to my regular grocery store (back then, I shopped almost entirely at the supermarket). I recommend you start wherever you usually do your grocery shopping, too. You're already familiar with the layout and the prices. Change can be unsettling and there is some comfort to be found in what we already know.

Ready? Let's go to the store! Allow yourself a bit of extra time for this shop. Or, if you prefer, you can choose not to shop at all. We're going to look at the store and the products they sell in a new light.

Starting at the entrance, make your way around the store as you normally would, and whenever you come to a product you'd usually buy, ask yourself the questions on the opposite page.

You don't have to find all the answers and you definitely don't have to make decisions about every single purchase. This is about finding easy swaps and better choices, but it's also about being aware of the areas where we could improve.

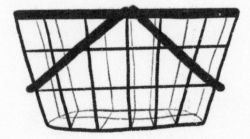

Where is it grown or made?	All products will state, somewhere, the country of origin. With unpackaged fruit and vegetables there may be a sticker with the country written on it; otherwise there will be a shelf label with the details. With packaged food, it will be printed somewhere on the label. This question gets us thinking about food miles: how far has this item travelled to get to our shopping basket?
How is it packaged?	When we buy the same things week in, week out, we often don't pay much attention to how they are packaged. It's just not on our radar ... until it is. Take your time looking at the packaging. Are there multiple layers – packets inside packets, or trays wrapped in plastic with cardboard outers? How much packaging is there relative to the actual product inside? What's it made of? This gets us thinking about whether the packaging is excessive, whether it's actually recyclable where we live and whether other products have better packaging options.
If it's a product, what ingredients does it contain?	Food manufacturers are required to list all ingredients on the label, with the ingredient used in the greatest amount listed first and the others following in descending order. This question gets us thinking about whether it's actually something we could make ourselves or substitute with a different product.
Could I choose better?	As you reflect on the things you usually buy, look at some of the alternatives. There are a lot of products on offer and it can feel exhausting to try to compare them all. Which is why, typically, we don't. We just buy the thing we always buy, or maybe the one on 'special offer'. So now is a great opportunity to step back, question our habits and ask ourselves: what is it that I'm currently buying, and can I do better?

part two

plastic and pre-packaged:
unwrapping
the solutions

what's all the fuss about:
plastic-free and zero waste?

Plastic packaging is increasingly harming wildlife, polluting our waterways and littering the environment. A recent study suggested that without action, there will be more plastic than fish in the ocean by 2050. There's a growing realisation that plastic shipped overseas for recycling is often not being recycled at all, and with more and more countries refusing to accept plastic for recycling, we're recognising that refusing and reusing are better options than recycling.

Plastic waste is a problem, but switching to different single-use materials is putting a lot of demand on other resources, which is why many people aim to reduce all single-use packaging.

Where we have the choice, no packaging at all is the least wasteful option.

Living with less waste is the philosophy of the zero-waste lifestyle movement. The movement started in 2008, when Bea Johnson began her blog, Zero Waste Home, detailing how her family avoided throwing anything in their landfill bin. Instead, they focused on refusing things they did not need, reducing, reusing – with recycling as the last resort.

The zero-waste ideal is both an empty landfill bin and an empty recycling bin. It's an ideal, not a reality (yet). For this to be possible we'd need a circular economy, where all resources are used and reused, recycled, remade and used again. The reality is that our economy is linear, and the systems and infrastructure we need to make zero-waste living truly attainable aren't yet in place. Instead of achieving perfection, zero-waste living means working towards reducing both landfill and recycling as much as is possible and practical.

Much of the single-use plastic packaging that we buy is food packaging. Refusing plastic starts here.

<u>More than 40 years</u> after the launch
of the first universal recycling symbol,
only 14 per cent of plastic packaging
is collected for recycling, and after
processing only 5 per cent is recycled.

Can I buy unpackaged?

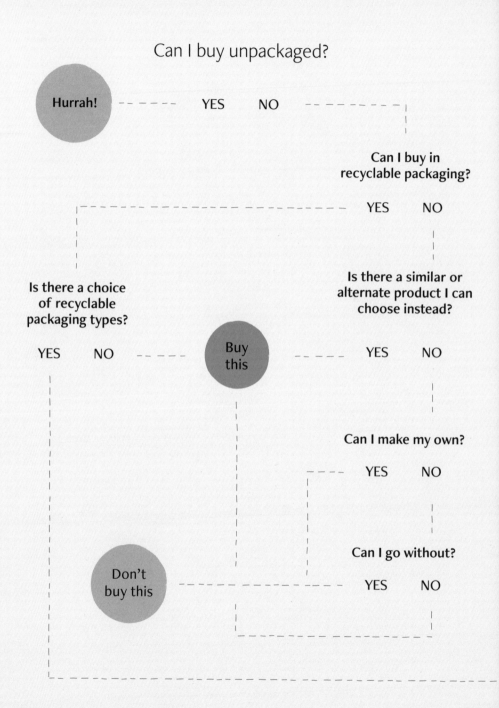

Hurrah!

YES   NO

Can I buy in
recyclable packaging?

YES   NO

Is there a choice
of recyclable
packaging types?

Is there a similar or
alternate product I can
choose instead?

YES   NO

Buy
this

YES   NO

Can I make my own?

YES   NO

Can I go without?

Don't
buy this

YES   NO

unpacking the packaging dilemma

If we can't buy something without packaging, our best option
depends on our priorities. From a carbon footprint perspective,
plastic is going to be better because it's lighter to transport;
but if you care more about plastic pollution and reducing your
waste footprint you might prefer a material like metal that is truly
recyclable. This flow chart will help you navigate the choices.
There's rarely a perfect solution and if you have limited options
that is in no way your fault. Make a choice, know you're doing
your best, and feel good about that.

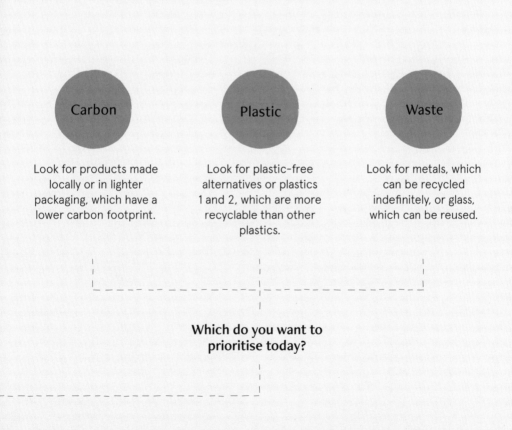

Carbon

Look for products made
locally or in lighter
packaging, which have a
lower carbon footprint.

Plastic

Look for plastic-free
alternatives or plastics
1 and 2, which are more
recyclable than other
plastics.

Waste

Look for metals, which
can be recycled
indefinitely, or glass,
which can be reused.

**Which do you want to
prioritise today?**

biodegradable and compostable plastics

What about plastic and packaging that uses claims like biodegradable, bioplastic, compostable and eco-friendly? There's often no agreed understanding or definition of what these terms mean, which makes it pretty confusing for us, the shoppers.

As you'll see from all the question marks in the table opposite, in many instances you can't actually tell from the label if something is made from plants, ocean-safe or truly compostable (so it's probably safer to assume not). Oxo-biodegradable plastic is made from fossil fuels, does not properly biodegrade and contributes microplastic pollution in the environment. Because oxo-biodegradable plastic offers no environment benefit, its use in single-use plastic products was prohibited in the EU in 2019.

If we're trying to avoid single-use packaging altogether, it's best to steer clear of this packaging too. If that's not doable, certified options are better because they have undergone independent testing to verify the claims.

Bioplastic is commonly derived from corn. It's sometimes called corn or cornstarch on the label, which sounds more natural than 'bioplastic'. Being derived from plants does not guarantee compostability.

what we know (and don't know) from the label

	Made from plants	Breaks down in the ocean	Breaks down in compost
Bioplastic	✓	?	?
Biodegradable	?	?	?
Oxo-biodegradable	x (made from fossil fuels)	x	x
Certified compostable	?	x	✓ (but only industrial compost)
Certified home compostable	?	?	✓
Eco-friendly or 'green'	?	?	?

what others do:
grocery shopping with less (or no) packaging

Many people start by switching from plastic to other, more recyclable materials: seeking out pasta or oats packaged in cardboard, olive oil and condiments like ketchup in glass, drinks in aluminium cans and longer-life foods in tins. Others, rather than seeking alternatives to plastic, try not to use packaging at all, or limit it as much as they can by seeking out places that sell groceries from self-service 'bulk' containers, where you bring and fill your own reusable bags or containers and buy only what you need (this type of shopping is called 'from bulk'). Some people have access to a bulk aisle at their supermarket, but more often avoiding packaging means shopping elsewhere. Some people commit to doing their entire grocery shop without packaging; others just buy a portion of their groceries this way.

Not everyone has access to bulk stores (although they are growing in popularity). Where there is no option to buy 'from bulk', some people choose to keep their waste down by buying 'in bulk'.

Shopping from bulk:

When we measure out and pay for exactly what we need of a particular ingredient, usually using our own containers or bags.

Shopping in bulk:

When we buy a wholesale quantity of a particular ingredient, and the ingredient is (usually) pre-packaged.

shopping at bulk stores

Bulk stores source products in bulk quantities from growers, producers and wholesalers and allow us, the customers, to buy exactly what we need from pre-filled 'bins' or dispensers. While most bulk stores provide single-use bags (usually paper) for customers to use, and may sell glass jars or other containers, the refilling of customers' own bags and reusing of containers is generally encouraged.

Bulk stores are also a great way to reduce food waste, because we can buy exactly what we need. There's no predetermined pack size, so if we only require two tablespoons for a recipe, that's all we need to buy. That's in sharp contrast to supermarkets, who set pack sizes and often make larger packs incrementally cheaper by weight, tempting us to buy more than we need; they also run frequent 'specials' and three-for-the-price-of-two deals to further encourage us to over-consume.

Bulk stores sell pantry items, particularly dry goods such as grains, flours, pulses, nuts, seeds, dried fruit, herbs, spices, baking ingredients and snacks. Many bulk stores also sell liquids: oils, vinegars, nut butters, sweeteners and sauces.

Bulk stores often refer to themselves as zero waste or plastic-free, meaning they are working towards these goals, as opposed to in a completely literal sense. One big 20-kilogram (44-pound) plastic container is less packaging than the equivalent in 100-gram (3.5-ounce) pre-packaged portions. Bulk stores usually take their recycling seriously and actively look for ways to reduce their packaging use.

Bulk store shopping is a very different experience to shopping at a supermarket. It's likely that the staff will be as enthusiastic about reducing waste as you, and will be delighted to answer questions. If you're unsure of anything, head straight to a staff member and explain that you're new to this way of shopping: ask how their store works and if there's anything you need to know.

questions to ask at bulk stores

Can I BYO containers?

As well as checking if BYO containers are permitted, you also need to find out if it's possible to deduct the weight of containers from a purchase. Most newer bulk stores are set up for this, but older stores don't always have suitable scales or systems and can't offer this service. If this is the case, use reusable produce bags that won't register on the scales. Produce bags are also a less cumbersome alternative if you don't have access to a vehicle.

Is weighing and labelling of containers self-service?

Depending on the store's policy, they may allow you to weigh and mark your own containers using scales provided (some will even print labels for your containers) or they may require a staff member to do it for you.

Are liquids sold by weight or volume?

With the exception of water, liquids do not have an equal weight and volume, and will be priced differently per kilo/pound and per litre/fluid ounce. If you're refilling your own container, it's important to pay attention to whether a liquid is priced per weight (you'll need to know the weight of the container) or by volume (you'll need to know the capacity of the container).

If you forget your own containers or don't have enough, the store probably has packaging available. It's worth remembering that resources are still required to produce this packaging. Paper bags have three times the carbon footprint of plastic ones, so simply replacing plastic bags with single-use paper ones every time isn't more sustainable. Try to save them for emergency purchases, and if you do need them, try to reuse them.

If we are used to supermarkets, we are used to unit prices, such as x price for a box of teabags, rather than price per kilo (or pound). This can be confusing at bulk stores, because we often don't have much idea what things weigh, which makes it hard to compare the cost. Loose-leaf tea, for example, may have an expensive kilo price, but is very lightweight. Sometimes stores provide scales for customers to use, so we can weigh a small amount to see how much it will cost before adding more. For the first few bulk store shops it will be helpful to get a receipt so you can compare with your normal place of shopping and your budget and make adjustments next time if things are wildly different.

To find your nearest bulk store, try an internet search engine, using terms such as 'plastic free shopping', 'zero waste grocery store' or 'bulk food store' and remember to include your town's name or your region. Social media is a great place to look too. The Zero Waste Home app has a map of bulk stores, but tends to be more US-centric.

containers to take bulk shopping

Old paper bags, zip-lock bags and plastic containers: just because they are touted as single use, that doesn't mean we have to limit ourselves to just one use.

Reusable mesh produce bags are suitable for any dry products excepting fine powders (flour, cocoa powder, etc.) – fabric bags are best for these.

There's no rule saying you have to fill your jar to the top! Two tablespoons, only half full or quarter full are all acceptable.

If you're using glass jars, stainless-steel containers and old Tupperware, there's no need to decant everything when you get home – simply pop the containers in the pantry.

bulk shopping online

If you don't live near a bulk store, it's sometimes possible to order groceries from a bulk store with online shopping and have them shipped without excess (or any) plastic. There's usually less flexibility with amounts, your order won't come packaging-free, and ordering online will have a bigger carbon footprint than buying from a physical store. However, if your local choices are limited, you're trying to source specific ingredients and avoid plastic, or you'd like to prioritise options not available in the physical stores where you live, online may be a workable alternative for you.

The country of origin and any organic certification should be clearly displayed for each ingredient or product listed. It will probably be less clear how the items are packaged for delivery; you might be able to find this information on the store website, or you might like to call or email to check.

Good questions to ask:

+ How will the groceries be packaged?
+ Is the packaging compostable, recyclable, reused and/or reusable?
+ Can packaging be returned for reuse?
+ How are the goods transported from store to door?

The great thing about small and independent businesses is that it is much easier to ask questions and get answers than from faceless corporations; they are often much more receptive to feedback and sometimes have the flexibility to accommodate requests.

Three stores that deliver groceries plastic-free:

+ **Australia:** The Source Bulk Foods, *thesourcebulkfoods.com.au*
+ **UK:** Plastic Free Pantry, *plasticfreepantry.co.uk*
+ **USA:** Azure Standard (Oregon), *azurestandard.com*

independent shops and food service counters

If there is no bulk store where you live, or the choice is limited, don't be disheartened. Other stores in your area – such as health food stores, independent grocers and small businesses – might not have a bulk section (although it is possible) but they will probably have different products packaged in different ways. In particular, you might find they sell certain ingredients packaged in larger quantities (which usually means less packaging overall). Asian supermarkets in particular often sell larger quantities of pulses and grains than are available at the supermarket.

Food service counters are found within larger supermarkets and also exist as independent businesses: delicatessens, bakeries, cheesemongers, butchers, fishmongers, hot food outlets and salad bars. They usually display a lot of unpackaged products; rather than use the single-use plastic and other packaging provided, it's often possible to bring your own containers and request that the assistant fills those instead.

No laws or regulations in Australia or the UK prohibit customers from bringing their own containers. However, stores may have their own policies. In Australia the big supermarkets are historically opposed to customers using their own containers, whereas in the UK many supermarkets are actively encouraging it. Independent businesses will often be very supportive.

Clean, lidded containers are ideal. Plastic tends to stain and scratch which makes it look unclean (and might lead to your container being refused), so use good-quality plastic or choose another material. Also, think about the products you'll be buying. Glass jars are great for deli items like olives, but their shape means they aren't going to work for everything.

When you try using your own containers for the first time, it's normal to feel a little nervous. It can be helpful to let anyone else waiting to be served go ahead of you so you don't feel like you have an audience or are holding anyone up. It will feel easier if you go to the store at a time when it's less busy, too.

When you're ready to order, *avoid asking if it's okay* for you to use your own containers. Instead, smile, look like you know exactly what you're doing, and tell the assistant, 'I'd like to use my own containers, I'm avoiding using single-use packaging'. It's good to explain your 'why' – you might think it is obvious, but that doesn't mean it is.

It's possible the assistant might refuse your request. More likely, they'll take your containers and tell you they think it's a great idea, or that you're the sixth person this week who's brought their own container. At least, that's been my experience.

You'll need to make sure they tare the weight of the scales (reset the weight to zero) before filling containers, or you'll be charged the weight of the containers too (and they are not light). Most staff will know how to do this. Just keep an eye on the scales and query it if the weight or price seems unusually high.

If the staff member does refuse your request, my first suggestion would be to look surprised. They might just be a little unsure, having not been asked this before. If you seem confident, like you do this all the time, they might reconsider. If they still say no, you could ask whether it's the store policy, or if it would be helpful if you spoke to the manager. Keep the conversation friendly and positive; they are just trying to protect themselves and keep their job. It's okay to feel disappointed but getting angry won't help. If you don't like the decision, find out who is making it, and try to engage them on the issue. Or, take your custom elsewhere.

Where bring-your-own containers aren't permitted, some people get around this by asking for their products to be wrapped in paper: they can be popped in containers once paid for to stop leakages on the way home.

buying in bulk

If you don't have access to a bulk store, you could consider buying some of your groceries *in* bulk. This is effectively what most bulk stores do – the difference is that they then allow customers to buy what they need *from* bulk; if you do it yourself, you're going to have to use it all yourself. It's often cheaper per kilo/pound than buying from bulk stores, but you have to be realistic about how quickly you'll be able to use the product up, and whether you've got adequate storage (both in terms of space and suitable conditions). Buying food at a less expensive price only for it to go mouldy, stale or get infested with weevils is a false economy; not only is it a waste of money but it's a waste of the resources we're trying to save.

If you can afford the upfront costs, and can store and will use what you buy, here are some options for finding groceries in bulk:

+ **Wholesale distributors:** some may require you to be a business to purchase from them, so check.
+ **Direct from farms or producers:** they will usually only have what they grow themselves, so you'll probably be restricted to one food group and maybe one product.
+ **Ordering online:** options include online grocery stores, directly from suppliers, and from wholesale distributors.

One way to reduce the risk of bulk food going bad before you get to eat it and also to lower the upfront costs is to find others to share with: simply join forces with a few friends, extended family members, colleagues or neighbours, and split the costs between you all. It can be a bit more work to shop this way but the food is usually cheaper and it's a great way to support growers and producers, source organic products and get access to better quality or fresher food.

Co-operatives (often called co-ops) are groups of people doing exactly this. Some are very informal and others are run more like businesses, but the principle is the same: to buy food in bulk and share the cost savings among members. The advantage of joining an existing co-operative is that they have already done a lot of the groundwork: they have relationships with suppliers and systems in place. To find out if there's a food co-operative in your area, ask the internet. Many informal co-ops won't have dedicated websites but they will usually have Facebook pages or groups. You may also find local community groups who can point you in the right direction.

If you can't find a local co-operative, you might think about starting one.

Divided equally between a few people, this will be less onerous than it might sound, and the member collection day can be a fun and social event that helps strengthen your local community. If you've got the passion, it's definitely something to consider.

how to start a co-op or food buying group

Step one
Ask friends, family, neighbours and colleagues if they'd be interested in joining and get some agreement before you begin researching.

Step two
Look at the prices of online stores, enquire at wholesalers and large suppliers and contact local farms to find out if it's possible to order online, whether there are minimum quantities, whether you'd need to pay in advance, and how much shipping is likely to be.

Step three
Use these figures to determine how much your members will need to commit to buying (and therefore how many members you'll require) to make it viable. It's best to discuss this with your potential members so they are aware of the costs and commitment.

Step four
Think about the number of tasks involved and how to share them among members. Some of the jobs you might need to allocate are:
+ Sending out order forms to members and collating orders
+ Placing orders with suppliers
+ Ensuring members pay for orders, and that suppliers are paid
+ Arranging a collection day where members pick up their orders
+ Measuring out individual orders from bulk deliveries

Step five
Think about suitable storage space (there will probably be at least a few days between order arrivals and member collections, and you might need to consider storing unsold items). Will you need a fridge or a freezer? You might need a separate area for unpacking and repacking member orders.

tweaking your purchases

Even if you can't commit to bulk shopping and you're restricted to your regular store, it is possible to make small changes that add up with time.

Look for less packaging	Take pasta, for example – the amount of packaging used varies considerably depending on the shape: spaghetti and macaroni use far less than vermicelli nests and pasta shells.
Look for bigger quantities	Rather than buying individual mini boxes of raisins or crackers, consider buying a larger packet and dividing it yourself.
Look for local	Maybe you've never noticed that the three brands of almond milk in the store come from three different countries and you could switch to the option with the least food miles. Or perhaps there's a different type of local plant milk that you could try.
Look for recyclable	Metals, cardboard and plastic numbers 1 and 2 are all more recyclable than other plastics. Mixed materials such as Tetra Paks (layers of cardboard, plastic and metal smooshed together) are particularly tricky to truly recycle and require specialist facilities to process.
Look for loose (and go for reusable)	Smaller reusable bags can be used for loose fruit and vegetables, or bread rolls or baked goods, and the bigger ones can be used to carry produce home. Some people choose to use paper mushroom or potato bags for all their loose produce, and a cardboard box to pop groceries into.

Packaging accounts for approximately 34 per cent of plastic use in the United States and 40 per cent of plastic use in Europe.

local less waste options:
for fresh produce

When it comes to fresh produce, there are often great local alternatives to the supermarket, so you can not only cut down on – or cut out – packaging, but reduce your food miles at the same time. Win win!

farmers' markets

Markets sell predominantly fresh food and specialty food products, and are distinguished from other community markets because the sellers are farmers, farm staff or specialty food makers.

Farmers' markets usually run in the morning on weekends and, depending on demand, may be weekly or bi-weekly, fortnightly or monthly. Some run year-round, and others only operate during specified months of the year. Some farmers will rotate across several markets and may only attend a specific market once a fortnight or once a month. Others will only attend during certain months when they have produce to sell (remember, many things don't grow all year round). You won't always be able to get the same things week in, week out; but the patterns of what is available each season will remain very similar from year to year. It often takes a few visits to get a good understanding of what is available.

Farmers' markets, unlike the big grocery stores, *want* to run out of things. So if you've got a specific shopping list or intend to do your entire grocery shop at the farmers' market, it pays to get there early.

Produce is often sold unpackaged at farmers' markets. If something has been packaged, you can ask the farmer if they can reuse the packaging; if it's a yes, decant the produce into your own reusable bag or container, and hand the packaging back. Farmers' markets are a great opportunity to raise concerns about packaging with the farmers; they may not have considered the issue before, or may have good reason (such as legislative requirements) to use packaging in a certain way, and be willing to discuss workarounds or other solutions with you.

Where to find your local farmers' market:

+ **Australia:** Australian Farmers' Market Association, *farmersmarkets.org.au*
+ **UK:** Farm Retail Association (also lists farm stores), *farma.org.uk*
+ **USA:** United States Department of Agriculture Agricultural Marketing Service, *ams.usda.gov/local-food-directories/ farmersmarkets*

Farm gate sales: some farmers sell produce (usually food) directly to customers through farm shops or roadside farm stands. Some operate pick-your-own systems where customers can pick their own fruit and/or vegetables at the farm.

vegetable box schemes

Vegetable box schemes deliver fresh vegetables and fruit to your doorstep (or a designated collection point) either directly from a farm or via a service that brings together the produce of several different farms. Often you can place an order online, and you'll usually have a choice of box size, and also frequency of delivery.

The offers from different companies vary. Some might only offer organic fruit and vegetables; others might specialise in 'ugly' or imperfect fruit and vegetables that aren't aesthetically pleasing enough to be sold at stores. You'll be given whatever is in season, although you might have different options, such as 'veg only' or 'fruit only'. Some offer other grocery items: pantry staples, dairy products and eggs. Different schemes will have different rules about choosing 'likes' and 'dislikes' – you may not have any choice, you may be able to nominate one or two, or you may have complete freedom. You may prefer supporting a hyper-local small producer, or the greater flexibility of a bigger company's scheme (even if that means more food miles).

If you're new to vegetable box schemes, it's worth trying out a few and seeing which works best for you. Even such things as delivery day can be an important factor – you might find a Thursday delivery (when your fridge is running low from the weekend) much more practical than a Monday delivery (when you are stocked up from the farmers' market the day before). You might think you're not fussy with food, but when you've received a cabbage in your box for three months straight it can be a relief to have the option to request cabbage-free boxes for a while. And how can you know you don't like celeriac if you didn't even know such a vegetable existed before it rolled up in your weekly vegetable box?

If you're not an experienced or confident cook, order a single smaller box as a trial. That way you can get a feel for where you need to plug gaps in your knowledge, and experiment with new (to you) ingredients. Increase the quantities and delivery frequency as you increase your skills in the kitchen.

local community food initiatives

Lots of us want to eat more locally grown food but too often
we don't think to stop and find out what's growing in our
neighbourhoods. Food, once we start looking, is everywhere.
What's more, people growing food are often happy to share
their excess – after going to all the trouble of growing it, the last
thing they want is to watch it go to waste. Taking a walk around
your neighbourhood might lead you to discover a mulberry tree,
a blackberry hedge or a box of free lemons by a neighbour's
letterbox, but if you're not too sure what you're looking for,
or even where to start, there are some great online resources
to help you on your search.

Urban fruit tree maps	Initiatives such as *fallenfruit.org* and *ripenear.me* map urban fruit trees, public orchards and community plantings as well as trees or shrubs on private land with surplus fruit.
Food swap groups	These informal neighbourhood groups share their excess food and produce at recurring events (often weekly, fortnightly or monthly). They run under a few different names, including Grow Swap Share groups and Crop Swap groups (find your local group at *foodswapnetwork.com* or, for Australian groups, *cropswap.sydney*).
Community fridges	Refrigerators located in public spaces, enabling free fresh food to be shared with the community. In the UK, a national network of community fridges has been set up by the environmental charity Hubbub with a goal of 100 open fridges by 2020.
Buy Nothing Project	A global network of community neighbourhood Facebook groups. It's only possible to join one group – the one where you live – and members can give, lend or take items including excess produce.
Food waste apps	Anyone with a smartphone can locate or share surplus food. Some apps are designed for home gardeners to share produce, others allow shoppers who purchased too much or bought something they didn't like to give the excess away, and some allow restaurants or cafes to sell food left at the end of the day at a discount. The best are those most utilised for your area: three popular apps are Olio, Too Good to Go and Bring Me Home.
Grow Free	Started in Australia and now expanding overseas, this network of sharing carts offers free home-grown produce, seeds and seedlings. Their listings can be found at *growfree.org.au*

community-supported agriculture

If you've been using vegetable box schemes for a while and are confident in the kitchen, you might like to consider community-supported agriculture (CSA). At first glance it's similar to a vegetable box scheme, but the approach is different.

CSA members usually purchase a share of a farm's annual harvest and agree to share the risk and also any surplus, which helps farmers manage their crops because they know demand. Customers commit for a period of time (which can range from a few weeks to several months, depending on the farm) and receive a box of produce every week. There may be a single upfront payment, or a few payments spread over a few months. There will usually be recipes accompanying the boxes, helping members use up the contents and avoid food waste. It's a movement focused on collaboration and commitment.

If you're dedicated to reducing your food miles, the CSA approach often has the lowest footprint of all. This system is more commonly used in the USA and Canada although it is growing in popularity in Australia and Europe.

The Open Food Network (OFN) is a global not-for-profit 'fair food' platform. It functions partly as an online directory, with producers, food hubs, farmers' markets, co-operatives and community food enterprises – no matter what size – able to create profiles which are added to a map. Any grower, producer or distributor has the option of setting up an online shop within the platform.

There are a growing number of local networks within the OFN. The first, the Australian Open Food Network, was established in 2012. There are currently networks in the UK, USA, France, Belgium, Germany, Scandinavia, Canada and South Africa, with more planned soon. Find out more at *openfoodnetwork.org*

grow your own

Growing some of your own fruit and vegetables is a great way to ensure what you eat is local and packaging free, not to mention it will taste much better than anything you buy in the shops and it's fun to do! Whether you have space to set up a veggie patch where the lawn used to be, or you only have a sunny windowsill with room for a few herbs in pots, growing your own is definitely something to consider.

If you're serious about growing your own, a good place to start is joining a local community garden. Not only will you share the work as well as the rewards, it's a great way to learn about what plants grow well in your local area and how the seasons affect what grows, and benefit from the knowledge of others in the group.

Where to find your local community garden:

+ **Australia:** Australian City Farms & Community Gardens Network, *communitygarden.org.au*
+ **UK:** Social Farms and Gardens, *farmgarden.org.uk*
+ **USA:** American Community Gardening Association, *communitygarden.org*

If you'd prefer to grow at home, starting small is going to be less overwhelming. A herb garden is a good place to begin, as a few herbs can add a lot of flavour to a meal, herbs can be expensive to buy from the store and they are rarely found without plastic. Plus, many herbs are very easy to grow. But if you really like beans, or potatoes, or strawberries, you might prefer to grow these instead. If you've got the space, fruit trees are also an option.

questions to ask when you're planning to grow food

What do I actually like to eat regularly?	You'd be amazed how often first-time gardeners grow something because it seems to be the thing that people grow, only to realise that they don't actually like it. It's also worth considering how much something costs to buy, because if you're limited on space and time, it makes more sense to grow food that is expensive to purchase.
When is the ideal time to plant this in my climate?	It's important to get growing advice for your climate, because things like soil temperature, the chance of frost, daylight hours and even which pests are prevalent at which times of year will all vary according to where you live. Most seeds and seedlings come with growing guidelines, but make sure they apply to your climate and conditions.
Is it better to sow seeds or transplant seedlings?	This depends on a few things. Seeds are usually cheaper to buy, but smaller seeds can be challenging to get going and usually take longer to produce food than their equivalent seedlings. Seedlings are more expensive but can be easier when you're starting out as the plants are already established. For slower-growing or frost-sensitive plants, seedlings extend the growing season and usually mean more produce. It is best to avoid root vegetable seedlings (carrots, beetroot, parsnips, radish) because the roots get damaged when the seedlings are transplanted – and the root is the bit you eat.
How long will this take to produce food?	Some plants take months to produce food (and trees can take multiple years to fruit), whereas others will be ready in a few weeks. Young salad leaves and leafy greens can be ready to pick in a few weeks; pumpkins/squash will need a few months.
How much will a single plant produce?	Some plants are prolific, and others not so much. Ideally you want enough to make a meal, but not so much you can't eat it all. Whereas one carrot seed will produce one carrot, a single tomato plant will produce several trusses of tomatoes, and a sole zucchini/courgette plant can probably pump out all the zucchini you'll need for a season. It's always useful to find out how much to expect per plant, and plan accordingly.

Consider buying as seedlings:

Thyme
Basil
Sage
Mint
Parsley
Capsicum/peppers
Strawberries

Easy to grow from seed:

Tomatoes
Beetroot
Beans
Radishes
Peas
Coriander/cilantro
Pumpkin/squash

Some plants require other related plants for pollination, so do check this – having a single plant won't always work in your favour.

overcoming obstacles:
if you're limited on budget

Learn to cook what's cheapest

Because we don't live in an ideal world, we may come up against challenges as we start to make changes to reduce our packaging use – but meaningful change is totally possible even with limitations.

If we'd like to buy more organic, shop at bulk stores and choose more local produce, but our budget restricts our freedom to make choices, we can prioritise the cheapest foods. If the three cheapest organic vegetables are onions, carrots and potatoes, we can look for more recipes that use these. If organic bread and wraps are expensive but organic flour is cheap, maybe we can make our own. If the cheapest grain at the bulk store is millet, perhaps now is the time to try cooking with it.

Sometimes we assume things are difficult to make simply because we are so used to buying them ready-made. But we'll never know if we don't try. That doesn't mean continuing to make them forever. But if something is easy, fun, saves money and you enjoy eating the result, why not? Don't forget that with bulk stores we have the option of buying exactly the amount we need for a recipe, so if it's a new ingredient, buy just enough.

Compare supermarket prices with bulk store prices

Sometimes people feel that they can't shop at bulk stores because they are too expensive, but it's extremely unlikely that everything will be more expensive. There is no rule that you have to do all of your grocery shopping at the bulk store, so find out which things are within your budget and choose to purchase what you can.

To know which is the cheapest option you'll need to know prices at your regular store and your local bulk store. If both offer online shopping, you'll be able to compare prices using a computer or your phone. It's more likely that your grocery store will have online shopping while the bulk store does not. If this is the case, make a note of the grocery store prices on your shopping list. The next time you go to the bulk store, take this list with you and compare the prices.

If neither store has an online option, you can find the prices on the shelf labels. When you're at the store, snap a picture of the price labels of the things you buy, keep your receipt and make a note of prices there.

Your store should display the price per weight. This is usually per kilo/ pound; however, if something has an expensive per kilo price the store might display the price as per 100 grams or even per 10 grams, so you might need to convert it in order to properly compare.

overcoming obstacles:
if you're limited on time

Choose one issue

When we're short of time, the best way to begin is by asking ourselves what we prioritise. We probably care about lots of things but choosing one to start with will free up some mental space and provide direction. Supporting local or switching out the plastic: which fires you up the most? In time you'll be able to expand your efforts to other issues.

Prioritise services and stores that save you time

Sometimes bulk stores allow customers to drop off their jars or containers along with a shopping list; staff then pack the order and the customer can pick it up and pay at the end of the day. Alternatively, you might like to try bulk store online shopping.

If you find it a challenge to get to the store mid-week, a vegetable box can be a convenient solution. If you're not up for the extra cooking challenge, consider looking for a scheme that offers a fruit-only box as a less waste, no fuss solution for snacks and lunch boxes. Many vegetable box schemes offer additional items, including fresh bread, eggs, dairy products and bulk goods.

Prepare and plan ahead

When we get busy, we tend to get forgetful. When it comes to remembering reusable shopping bags or reusable produce bags, rather than keeping them stashed in a drawer, hang them by the front door as a visual reminder. Write a reminder on the top of your shopping list. If you often find yourself at the store without reusable bags, is it easier to simply keep a set in the car? Or would it be better if you invested in some small and light enough to fit in your handbag (if you carry one), so you're always prepared?

For most of us, making changes is not about a complete life overhaul. It's about tweaking the routines and habits we already have. This can be tricky at first, but as we start to learn all the options, we can slot them into our schedule. As we learn that there's a great bakery next to the school, or a bulk store with late-night opening that we drive past after work, we can start to adjust our day to fit these trips in and avoid making separate ones. Markets often make for great socialising opportunities, so consider combining a market trip with catching up with friends.

There's always time ...

Our available time often ebbs and flows over the course of the year, or from year to year. If you're having a particularly busy time of it and need to step back, do what you need to do. Maybe that means getting more takeaway or embracing convenience for a while. Maybe we notice that being busier than usual means we're forgetting the reusables more often, or there's more food going to waste in the fridge. No one is perfect, and no one does all of the things all of the time. When you notice there's space in your life to do more, you can do more.

If you're thinking that going to two different shops sounds like twice the work, remember that bulk stores sell long-life items. With a bit of organisation you might only need to pop in there once every few months.

part three

counting carbon:
climate-friendly
food choices

what's all the fuss about: animal products?

With predictions that the world population will reach 10 billion people by 2050, we need to think differently about how (and what) we eat.

The reason that reducing meat and other animal products is so widely discussed as a way of lowering our individual environmental footprint is that while all farming has an impact, producing meat and animal products has the highest of all.

As our global population has increased, so has the population of animals raised to feed us, and the land required to grow crops to feed them. The food system that was sustainable for centuries has quickly tipped out of balance and is now responsible for one quarter of greenhouse gas emissions globally, with animal products counting for more than half of this.

Two significant contributors are beef (including dairy cattle) and lamb. Part of the reason is that cows and sheep are both ruminants, releasing methane after digestion of food; another factor is deforestation to create grazing pasture or to grow feed.

Many people ease into reducing their meat consumption by starting out with a simple challenge, such as participating in Meat-free Monday, a not-for-profit initiative launched by Sir Paul, Stella and Mary McCartney. A 2015 study concluded that a diet that limits meat consumption to two days a week would reduce carbon emissions by almost half compared with eating meat every day.

Meat, aquaculture (farming fish and crustaceans), eggs and dairy use around 83 per cent of the world's farmland, contribute 56–58 per cent of food's carbon emissions, provide 37 per cent of our protein and 18 per cent of our calories.

what others do:
reducing meat consumption

Cutting animal products completely from our diet can reduce our carbon footprint from food by two thirds. Even reducing animal product consumption by small amounts has an environmental benefit.

There are a number of ways that people try to lower their footprint by reducing animal products, and a number of 'diets' that reflect these lifestyle choices.

Not all of these names roll off the tongue, but they can be useful when trying to direct our personal moral compass or explain our choices to others. If you like having a simple set of rules to follow, you may like these options. You may realise that you fall under different labels under different circumstances, and that a combination works for you. Or you may decide that such labelling isn't helpful for you. You choose what you eat, and you also get to choose what you call (or don't call) yourself.

There may be other, unrelated reasons why people choose to follow a particular diet, including allergies, taste preferences, health benefits, weight management or the ethical treatment of animals. Here, we are simply exploring these diets in the context of environmental footprint.

There is more carbon dioxide in the atmosphere than any other greenhouse gas, and it sticks around longer than the others. Methane, nitrous oxide and other greenhouse gas emissions are converted to their carbon dioxide equivalents when calculating carbon footprints.

lower footprint diets

Climatarian
Considering the carbon footprint of food choices, particularly the types and quantity of meat and dairy products eaten, and shifting to those that have a smaller footprint. The climatarian diet suggests that as a minimum, consumption of beef and lamb be reduced to one standard serving (65 grams or 2.3 ounces) a week, or one large serving a month (300 grams or 10 ounces). As a next step, cutting out beef and lamb altogether is suggested, as is limiting consumption of cheese (which has the highest carbon footprint of all dairy products).

Flexitarian
Also called a semi-vegetarian diet, this is eating mostly plant-based foods, but with the flexibility to consume meat, seafood and other animal products (such as dairy and eggs) in moderation. Overall, the goal is to eat more nutritious plant-based foods and less meat.

Reducetarian
The vision is a world where consumption of meat, seafood and animal products is significantly reduced, but instead of adopting an all-or-nothing approach, individuals are encouraged to do what they can and contribute to collective change.

Vegetarian
Choosing not to eat meat or seafood, and eating a diet of plant-based foods and some animal products, including dairy, eggs and honey.

Plant-based
Choosing to predominantly eat plant foods including fruits and vegetables, grains and legumes, nuts and seeds, with an emphasis on unprocessed or minimally processed foods. Most people on a plant-based diet limit or avoid animal products.

Vegan
Choosing not to eat any animal products at all, including meat and seafood, all dairy products, eggs and honey (which is made by bees and not considered vegan).

staying healthy on a plant-based diet

Some people worry that switching to a vegetarian or vegan diet will mean that they don't get the nutrients that they need to stay healthy. Of course, eating meat and animal products is no guarantee of getting all the nutrients we need to stay healthy either – there are plenty of unhealthy people eating a meat-rich diet high in processed and fast food. But there are certain nutrients more available in animal products, and no one wants to change their diet to the detriment of their own health.

It is fairly easy to get all of our protein needs from plants. It is also possible to get enough iron, calcium and zinc from plant-based sources, although it requires a balanced and varied wholefood diet, alongside understanding how these minerals can be better absorbed. Some vegetarians and vegans choose to take supplements. Vitamin B12 is not readily available in plant-based foods, and B12 supplements are recommended for vegetarians and vegans.

Reducing is different from eliminating. The best thing to do if you're planning on changing your diet significantly or have concerns is to consult a healthcare professional, who can check your blood levels of things like B12 and iron, monitor changes and provide advice tailored to your needs.

A 2017 study by the journal _Nature_ found that to keep climate change at under 2 ˚C, the average world citizen needed to eat 75 per cent less beef, 90 per cent less pork and half the number of eggs, and citizens of rich nations including the UK and USA needed to cut dairy milk consumption by 60 per cent.

protein from plants

Humans are made up of proteins, and we need them for our cells to function. The building blocks of proteins are amino acids. Our bodies can make some amino acids, but we get nine solely from dietary protein. These nine are called essential amino acids: any protein source that has all nine is called a complete protein.

The recommended daily intake for protein can be calculated based on weight. For 'average' adults aged nineteen to seventy, the Australian National Health and Medical Research Council estimates the recommended daily intake of protein (in grams) by multiplying body weight (in kilograms) by 0.75 gram for women, and by 0.84 gram for men. Protein needs change with age and other life circumstances, such as pregnancy.

Almost all animal products are complete proteins, but the protein content of different plant foods varies significantly. If you're reducing your animal protein, you'll want to include higher-protein plant foods in your diet. Most plants are not complete proteins, usually missing one or more of the essential amino acids. A diet with a variety of different grains, legumes and vegetables can provide all the essential amino acids over the course of the day.

Many animal proteins can be substituted directly with plant protein in recipes (tofu for chicken, or lentils for ground mince).

plants with complete proteins

Amaranth

Small, round seeds that are cooked before eating. An ancient 'pseudo-grain' (see page 158 for more on grains), it has been cultivated for 8000 years and is gluten free.

Buckwheat

Grain-like seeds that can be used in the same way as other cereals. Despite the name buckwheat is neither a wheat nor a grass (it's actually related to rhubarb), and it is gluten free.

Chia seeds

Tiny black or white edible seeds from a flowering plant in the mint family that can be eaten raw or cooked.

Hemp seeds

These can be found hulled (with the outer fibrous shell removed, sometimes called hemp hearts) or whole. Hemp seeds are soft with a mild, nutty flavour and can be eaten raw or cooked.

Soy (including edamame beans, tofu and tempeh)

A protein-rich legume, sometimes called soya. Soybeans require cooking or fermentation to make them digestible. Edamame beans, the immature fresh green pods, are boiled or steamed before serving, tofu is boiled and pressed, and tempeh is fermented.

Quinoa

Another pseudo-grain, quinoa is related to spinach and is a round seed (which can be red, white or black), larger than amaranth. It is also gluten free.

plant foods high in protein

Pseudograins

Amaranth, buckwheat, quinoa

Nuts

Peanuts, almonds, pistachios

Seeds

Hemp seeds, pumpkin seeds,
sunflower seeds, sesame
seeds and tahini

Pulses

Puy lentils, split red lentils,
green lentils, mung beans

Other

Tofu and other soy products,
goji berries, nutritional yeast

calcium from plants

Calcium is the most abundant mineral in our bodies. We need it for strong bones and healthy teeth, but it also helps our blood clot and muscles contract. We often associate dairy products with calcium (although some seafood is also a good calcium source), but there are many plant foods rich in calcium too.

Nuts

Raw almonds (skin on),
raw Brazil nuts

Seeds

Sesame seeds and tahini,
chia seeds, fennel seeds

Dried fruit

Figs, goji berries

Vegetables

Kale, collard greens,
basil, parsley

Other

Tofu and other soy products,
cinnamon

iron from plants

Humans need iron to maintain healthy blood cells. There are two types of iron in food: haem iron (derived from meat, fish and poultry) and non-haem iron (derived from dairy and plant sources). Non-haem iron is not as readily absorbed as haem iron, but absorption can be improved: for example, by cooking greens rather than eating them raw, and combining with vitamin C (by adding a squeeze of lemon juice to the dish).

Seeds

Pumpkin seeds, hemp seeds

Pulses

Red, green and Puy lentils

Dried fruit

Goji berries, apricots,
currants, sundried tomatoes

Vegetables

Mature English spinach,
silverbeet/Swiss chard

Other

Cocoa powder

switching animal products

Cutting down on animal products isn't for (or of interest to) everyone. Instead, some people choose to reduce consumption of particular products without decreasing animal product consumption overall.

+ Switching from beef, lamb and pork to poultry (including chicken, turkey, duck and game birds such as pheasant) means a lower carbon footprint.
+ In Australia, kangaroo is considered a more sustainable meat, in part because kangaroos are naturally free-range and do not require feeding with grain.
+ Purchasing poultry cuts with the skin and bones included uses more of the bird. The bones can be kept and used to make stock or bone broth.
+ Choosing 'forgotten' or less popular cuts makes better use of an animal, and helps reduce overall demand.
+ Soft (less dense) cheeses including ricotta, cottage cheese, cream cheese, brie, gorgonzola and feta have a lower carbon footprint than hard cheeses because they take less milk to produce.
+ Sheep's milk has almost double the fat content of cow's milk, and a lower water content, meaning less milk is required to make sheep's cheese than an equivalent cheese made of cow's milk.

One reason why some people choose to eat animal products is that they live in communities or climates where animals are farmed (sometimes these places are not suited for other types of agriculture) and prefer to support local farmers. Choosing locally produced food cuts down on carbon emissions needed for transportation and connects us to our community.

<u>Beef and lamb often make their way into
pet food</u>. Switching to poultry, rabbit or
fish – whether in the form of kibble or fresh
meat – is a lower carbon footprint solution.
Rather than buying popular cuts of meat
from the butcher for a pet, consider less
desirable (to humans) options such as
chicken necks and chicken frames,
and offal (such as liver).

what's all the fuss about: organic?

Organic food is produced using organic farming practices, which means it is grown without chemical fertilisers or synthetic pesticides. We often think of organic food as being a health-conscious choice, but that's just one part of it. Organic farming has benefits for the land, the wildlife and the people who live nearby; it works with nature rather than against it.

Organic farms use sustainable systems and practices: improving soil health and fertility rather than depleting it, using natural fertilisers such as manure and compost, and rotating crops. They also encourage natural predators (such as birds) to control insect pests by maintaining hedgerows and trees in the fields. Organic animal products are produced without routine use of antibiotics and growth hormones.

Organic farming is not a new concept: it is how indigenous people and farmers have worked the land for centuries. It was only after World War II that farming changed, becoming increasingly intensive and reliant on chemicals. Nitrogen left over from making bombs was given a new use making fertiliser. Hedgerows and trees were removed to make way for tractors, which also removed natural predators and meant more need for pesticides and increased soil erosion (which increased the need for fertilisers). Many of these fertilisers and chemicals are water soluble so they don't stay on the farm; they get washed into rivers and streams where they unbalance natural systems. The introduction of factory farming, where huge numbers of animals are crammed into tiny spaces, meant disease and infection spread more easily and led to the routine introduction of antibiotics.

Thinking about carbon footprints, chemical fertilisers use huge amounts of fossil fuels – they are both made of them and use them in the manufacturing process. The Haber-Bosch process, an industrial process that creates nitrogen fertiliser, produces around 450 million tonnes (992 billion pounds) of carbon dioxide emissions every year. That's more than any other chemical-making reaction. Fertiliser production also releases large amounts of carbon dioxide. On farms, ammonia fertilisers are linked to another, more potent greenhouse gas: nitrous oxide.

Whereas conventional agriculture relies heavily on fossil fuels, organic farming not only reduces fossil fuel consumption by avoiding chemical fertilisers, but has been shown to increase soil carbon through the use of natural fertilisers.

Many of us struggle with the idea of buying everything organic, even when we agree that it is better, because almost always, organic means more expensive. In many ways this needs reframing: the reality is that industrially farmed and processed food is often artificially cheap. The reason 'conventional' non-organic produce is cheaper is that the price doesn't reflect the real cost – particularly the cost to the environment.

The amount we spend on groceries has steadily declined over the last 100 years. (Before 1920, a US family spent more than 40 per cent of their income on food. By 1960 the average American spent 17 per cent of their income on food, and this has continued to decline to less than 10 per cent today, of which half is eating out.) But that's not to say the money we no longer spend on groceries is just sitting there in a pot: we've often committed it to something else. So where switching to a wholly organic diet might blow the grocery budget, many people choose to start small. It's never all or nothing.

Externalised costs: when the costs of production are paid not by the producer or the purchaser but someone else. Examples include not paying workers a living wage, and the pollution of waterways with chemical run-off, which the community or government then bear the cost of cleaning up.

<u>Critics of organic farming</u> say that because yields are lower, we need more land to produce the same amount of food. But this assumes 'business as usual'. Rather than using more land, it would be much more sustainable to find ways to stop one third of all the food we produce going to waste.

the dirty dozen and the clean fifteen

Every year the US-based Environmental Working Group (EWG) put out a report called the 'Shopper's Guide to Pesticides in Produce'. They analyse more than 40,000 samples of popular fruits and vegetables and rank them according to their contamination with pesticides. The produce is tested as it would be eaten – so peeled and washed if that is how it would be prepared at home.

From this, the EWG produces two lists: the Dirty Dozen, the twelve foods found to have the highest levels of pesticide residue; and the Clean Fifteen, the fifteen foods with the lowest (if any) detected pesticide residues. The idea is that shoppers can feel informed about pesticide exposure and what benefits choosing organic might have (both for our own health and that of the environment).

Of course, the 'Shopper's Guide' isn't perfect. The USDA doesn't test every food every year, and samples are exactly that: samples. Different growers will use different amounts of different pesticides. An important thing to realise is that they are testing food sold in the USA. If you live outside the USA, you wouldn't expect the same results, because different pests occur in different areas, and different chemicals are allowed (or not). For example, the most frequently detected pesticide, found on 60 per cent of kale samples, was Dacthal/DCPA – classified by the US Environmental Protection Agency since 1995 as a possible human carcinogen and banned for use in Europe since 2009. Dacthal is not banned in Australia.

Critics of the report claim it is created to scare us, and discourages eating fresh fruit and vegetables. I disagree. I think it gives those of us concerned about the environment and the impacts of intensive agricultural practices a place to start. If we can't switch to organic everything, knowing the worst offenders allows us to swap out the things that will have the biggest impact.

dirty dozen 2019

Strawberries

Spinach

Kale

Nectarines

Apples

Grapes

Peaches

Cherries

Pears

Tomatoes

Celery

Potatoes

clean fifteen 2019

Avocados

Sweetcorn

Pineapples

Frozen sweet peas

Onions

Papayas

Eggplants

Asparagus

Kiwi fruit

Cauliflower

Cantaloupe/
rockmelon

Broccoli

Mushrooms

Honeydew melons

beyond the dirty dozen: cereals

As we discussed earlier, chemical fertilisers are a huge burden on the environment, both in terms of the fossil fuels they consume and the greenhouse gases they release. While the Dirty Dozen and the Clean Fifteen reports focus on pesticide residues, vegetables are actually the most heavily fertilised of all arable and permanent crop groups worldwide. It's not just pesticide use we reduce when we switch to organic but chemical fertiliser use too.

Cereals are not the most heavily fertilised food crops, but they cover more than half of the world's harvested area. Most of us eat grains every day. Knowing which are particularly heavy feeders can help us to make swaps that will lead to better outcomes for the planet.

Of all the cereals, corn, wheat and rice use the most fertilisers, so choosing organic would have a bigger relative impact. Oats, sorghum and millet have lower fertiliser needs than their greedy cousins: if organic isn't an option, consider choosing to eat more of these.

More than half of the world's calories are provided by just three crops: rice, maize and wheat.

what's all the fuss about: palm oil?

Palm oil isn't something most of us have ever seen on the shelves (it's pretty hard to buy as an ingredient) but it's actually the most widely consumed vegetable oil on the planet. It is produced from the fruit of tropical oil palms (a type of palm tree). Palm kernel oil is a different oil from the same trees – produced from the seed, not the fruit. Generally, palm oil is used in food, and palm kernel oil is used in non-edible products such as soap, cosmetics and detergents. It is estimated that half of supermarket products contain palm oil.

Palm oil is one of the few highly saturated vegetable fats; this means it is naturally semi-solid at room temperature. Raw palm oil can be refined into both a liquid and a solid, and it is tasteless. The liquid oil is often used in baked or fried products (in its raw state it is red, so it makes products appear more 'golden'), and to improve the texture of products like peanut butter, mayonnaise and ice cream. The solid fat is used in baked goods and pastry as a cheaper (and dairy-free) alternative to butter, in chocolate and desserts as a much cheaper alternative to cocoa butter, and in dairy-free spreads.

Oil palm trees produce more oil from less land than any other oil crop (five times more than rapeseed and olive oil, six times more than groundnut and sunflower oil, and more than ten times soy bean and coconut oil crops). The trees also fruit continuously, and production costs are lower than for other oils. Many see palm oil as an efficient and profitable crop.

It's no wonder then that demand for palm oil has exploded. In 2019–2020, 75 million tonnes (165 billion pounds) of palm oil were produced worldwide, with 84 per cent coming from Indonesia and Malaysia. Oil palms take up around 10 per cent of the world's permanent crop land.

What does this have to do with waste and carbon? Lots. Palm oil is the sixth most heavily chemically fertilised crop in the world – and those fertilisers are made from fossil fuels, and release greenhouse gases.

Demand for palm oil has meant a significant amount of deforestation, displacement of indigenous people and wildlife habitat loss as old rainforest is cleared to make way for new plantations. Clearing of peatlands and planting of oil palms in these areas increases the risk of fire, and the UN suggests peatland fires contribute around 5 per cent of human-caused carbon emissions. Orangutans are particularly threatened by palm oil production, but the Sumatran elephant, tiger and rhino, the Bornean pygmy elephant, and the humans who live in these areas all are threatened by palm oil plantations.

The Roundtable on Sustainable Palm Oil (RSPO) was established in 2004 to promote the growth and use of sustainable palm oil products. It now has over 4000 members worldwide and has developed a set of criteria that companies must comply with in order to produce certified sustainable palm oil (CSPO). The RSPO currently certify about 20 per cent of global palm oil production; however, many consider the standards to be weak and enforcement limited.

<u>Identifying palm oil on labels</u>: a European Union law on food information that came into force in 2014 requires that palm oil must be clearly labelled as palm oil; it cannot be called vegetable oil (this requirement does not extend to non-food products like shampoo, soap or cosmetics). The US Food and Drug Administration (FDA) requires that oils be declared by their common or usual name in food products. In Australia there is no such requirement and palm oil can be labelled as vegetable oil.

how others reduce or avoid palm oil

Choose certified sustainable palm oil	Check product packaging for the CSPO logo or a declaration, or check the manufacturer's website.
Avoid palm oil and find alternatives	Read the labels of products and switch to those that don't contain palm oil (when unsure, check the company's website or send an email to confirm). To avoid liquid palm oil, choose products that use alternatives such as sunflower oil, olive oil or rapeseed oil. Solid palm oil is trickier because very few edible oils are solid at room temperature. Butter is the traditional option, but if you're avoiding dairy, coconut oil or cocoa butter are alternatives (they have their own environmental footprints but are thought to be less harmful than palm oil).
Do without	Where there's no alternative that's free from palm oil, making the product from scratch can be an option. Others find that the easiest way to avoid palm oil is to avoid packaged processed foods altogether.

The issues caused by the clearing of land for palm oil plantations in Indonesia and Malaysia are mirrored in the clearing of rainforest in South America for cattle grazing and soy production (it is estimated that 70–90 per cent of the world's soybean crop is used as animal feed).

what's all the fuss about:
seasonal produce?

Seasonal produce means fruit and vegetables that are harvested locally when growing conditions are at their peak and the plants are most productive. When produce is in season it is usually at its most flavoursome. Generally, the foods that grow in a particular season are also the kinds of foods we want to eat in that season. For example, cucumbers, lettuce and tomatoes all grow best in summer when we are more likely to be eating salads. In winter, root vegetables and more robust vegetables like cauliflower and leeks lend themselves to warming soups and stews.

By contrast, out-of-season produce is fruit or vegetables that do not grow naturally in that season in the location where they are being sold. Out-of-season produce can sometimes be grown locally with a little bit of 'help': by using artificial light and heating to create the preferred conditions of a plant. For example, tomatoes need a soil temperature of at least 15 °C (60 °F) to grow and bear fruit, and may be grown in heated greenhouses outside of the summer months to produce a crop. These greenhouse tomatoes have a higher carbon footprint than seasonal field-grown tomatoes.

Alternatively, produce can be picked in one part of the world where it is in season, and transported to a country where it is not. This can mean picking produce before it is truly ripe, so that it transports better (ripe fruit especially bruises easily). Picking unripe can impact taste, particularly with fruits that benefit from sun-ripening (such as stone fruit).

If we're used to shopping at the supermarket, sticking to a regular shopping list and rotating the same recipes, it's likely that we are pretty detached from seasonal produce. It can take time to familiarise ourselves with what's in season and how to cook with it – but once we do, our food will always taste better.

<u>A locavore</u> is someone striving to only
or primarily eat food that is produced
locally, usually taken to mean within about
160 kilometres (100 miles) of its point of
purchase or consumption. Some locavores
avoid all ingredients not produced locally;
others permit dried goods or foods they do
not want to live without.

Around the world, there will be variations in the varieties and even quantities of produce available. Eating seasonally is often easier in certain climates, or at particular times of the year. For some people, their only option is the local supermarket. The best way to shop seasonally at the supermarket is to check the 'country of origin' labels and choose the produce that is grown closest to home. Even when we know what to expect to be in season, it's still worth reading the labels: supermarkets sometimes sell imported produce even when that same produce is in season and available locally.

For those that have the option, buying directly from farmers is a very seasonal way to eat (refer back to page 62 for ways to do this). This is an opportunity not only to reduce the food miles of the groceries we buy, but to support our local farmers. It often means less packaging; plus, when we're buying directly from a farmer or producer, it's a lot easier to have a conversation about alternatives and potentially influence change.

part four

food not waste:
keeping groceries
out of landfill

focus on food waste

It's been estimated that the average Australian household throws away 20–25 per cent of everything they buy. Imagine, every time you went shopping, putting four grocery bags on the kitchen counter and the fifth one, still packed, in the bin. We all think we don't waste food, but these figures come from somewhere! The thing about averages is that at least half of us are below them.

If you want to reduce what you throw away, a bit of forward planning before you head to the store will go a long way. Every shopping trip is a new opportunity to do better!

avoid food waste (and stretch your budget)

Shop your fridge (and freezer, and pantry)

Have a good look to see exactly what you already have. This will not only stop you buying duplicates or more than you need, but it also makes it easier to buy ingredients that complement what you have at home.

Plan meals (a little)

Planning meals a few days ahead is helpful, but if you don't normally plan, don't go overboard. A lengthy, rigid meal plan that you don't stick to just wastes food. Check your calendar, and only buy food for meals you will be having at home. If you have a busy week ahead it might be better to plan to make a big batch of something so you have leftovers, rather than trying to be creative.

Make a list

Having a list is a lot easier than trying to remember everything when we get to the shop. Without a list we're much more likely to buy things on impulse or to buy things we already have, and spend more money overall. Don't forget to add a reminder to take your reusable bags and containers to the list!

Check your food waste diary

If you've been keeping a food waste diary (see page 33), have a look through it to remind yourself what you threw away since you last went shopping, and why. Don't automatically replace what went bad. Have a break and see if you miss it.

Don't shop when hungry

When we go shopping hungry, we tend not only to buy more food, but also more junk food. We make better buying decisions when we've eaten, so put off the shopping trip until then.

Know your storage

Misconceptions about food safety are some of the key reasons why people throw perfectly edible food in the bin.

food safety: an overview

Use-by dates

In Australia, New Zealand, Europe and the UK, use-by dates are about safety – they are used to specify how long food can be kept until it begins to deteriorate, and food that has exceeded its use-by date cannot legally be sold because it may pose a health risk. Typically, use-by dates are used for foods that go bad quickly or are associated with a higher risk of food poisoning: meat, fish, pre-prepared fruit and vegetables, and some dairy products.

However, in the USA, a use-by date (sometimes printed on the packaging as 'best if used by') is not a safety date, with the single exception of infant formula; it simply means the last date recommended to use the product while at peak quality. In Canada, use-by dates are not used on any product except pre-packaged fresh yeast.

Best-before dates

Best-before dates are not concerned with safety. Rather, they indicate that food quality will be at its best before the specified date, but the food should still be safe to eat after it has passed. There may be some decline in flavour or texture. Food can still legally be sold after this date, as long as it is still fit for human consumption and has been stored correctly (in the refrigerator, for example, for chilled products).

Best-before dates are used for a variety of foods, including pre-packaged fresh fruit and vegetables, bread, pantry items such as dried pasta or chocolate, and frozen food.

In Australia, any food product with a shelf life of two years or longer (such as canned food) is not required to be labelled with a best-before date; bread products with a shelf life of less than seven days may have a 'baked on' date instead.

'Display until' and 'sell by' dates

These dates are sometimes used by stores for stock management purposes, and have absolutely nothing to do with food safety or quality. They are designed for store employees, not shoppers.

Food spoilage v. food poisoning

When food has spoiled, we know about it. We can see or smell it: sour milk, unpleasant-smelling yoghurt, furry fruit, slimy vegetables, mouldy bread. Spoiled food tastes 'off' too: rancid nuts taste bitter and unpleasant and you'll want to spit them out. Food that has spoiled isn't fit to eat.

On the other hand, food poisoning is mostly caused by pathogens that don't usually affect the taste, smell or appearance of food. Common culprits include salmonella, E. coli and campylobacter bacteria and norovirus, and infection is often linked to poor hygiene. Food is contaminated by these pathogens when handled by or in contact with infected people, faecal matter, infected water, and people who have been handling animals.

Food poisoning tends to occur when food hasn't been stored or cooked properly. Foods that have use-by dates are those that are most likely to be carrying the bacteria that cause food poisoning, but it isn't a guarantee that they do: beef, dairy, eggs and poultry tend to be higher risk than other foods.

10 per cent of the 88 million tonnes (194 billion pounds) of food waste created in the EU is linked to date marking.

no label, no problem

When we purchase food that's packaging free, there are no dates printed on the product label because there are no labels.

+ With unprepared fruit and vegetables, food poisoning risks are low. We can trust our judgement and give everything a good wash before eating.
+ With prepared products, and anything purchased from a food service counter, storage instructions are often displayed or printed alongside a use-by or best-before date on the price label. Alternatively, we can ask the food service assistant for advice.
+ Bulk goods most likely arrived at the store with a best-before date that is usually displayed on the ticket. If in doubt as to the freshness/age of a product, check with staff.
+ We can limit the risk of food poisoning by washing hands, keeping utensils and kitchen surfaces clean, washing food before preparing it and ensuring it is thoroughly cooked. (E. coli and salmonella are both killed at 70°C/160°F.)
+ Leftovers can be kept in the fridge for 3–7 days (anything free from meat, fish, eggs or dairy is lower risk).

It's hard to write about food safety guidelines when I know I've broken pretty much every rule that I'm telling you. I've eaten plenty of things past their use-by dates. After all, something that's considered safe to eat at 11.59 pm on the use-by day doesn't suddenly tick over to unsafe at 12.01 am. I've scraped off bad bits and lived to tell the tale. I routinely leave (plant-based) leftovers in the fridge for a week. If something is past its use-by date or leftovers have been in the fridge for an extended period, I ensure I cook it thoroughly before eating. I know where I source my food and I know which foods are most associated with food poisoning; I'm not young, old, pregnant, taking medication or immunocompromised, and I take the risk. I'm not going to encourage you to do the same, but it's worked out so far for me.

<u>Reviving produce</u>: don't confuse bad with sad. Place limp lettuce leaves and bendy carrots in a bowl of icy cold water for 30 minutes. Revive leafy greens, herbs, or vegetables with a distinct stalk (like broccoli) by placing the stems in a glass of water.

<u>Test your eggs</u>: to find out if your eggs are safe to eat, test them in a bowl of water. If they lie flat on the bottom they are fresh; if they start to point upwards, or appear to be standing upright, they are fine to eat but need to be prioritised: if they float to the top, they're probably past their best. (The Egg Safety Center in the USA suggests that buoyancy does not automatically mean the egg is bad, and it can be cracked into a bowl and checked for 'off' odour or unusual appearance before deciding whether or not to use it.)

glass jars

Generally speaking, clear containers such as glass jars are better for storing food, because you can see exactly what's inside. This helps with meal planning and to reduce duplicate purchases.

When I switched over to a low-waste kitchen, I found there was no need for me to go out and buy brand new glass jars or storage containers. I was able to repurpose glass jars I already had, and friends and family gave me glass jars that were heading to their recycling bins. I sourced all my extra-large glass jars from a local cafe that would otherwise have thrown them away, and I found a few useful jars at the charity shop. For me, reducing my waste is more about reusing resources that already exist over buying new; however, if you know that a hundred mismatched lids will give you anxiety, or that having an ordered pantry is the only way you can make this work for you, then do what you need to. Whatever you decide, choose the best quality you can afford and look after everything you buy.

removing old stickers

It makes for a less confusing pantry or fridge if you remove the old food labels from your jars (unless you're refilling with the same thing). Some jar labels just peel off, and others will dislodge after a soak in warm water. For more stubborn labels, apply a thin layer of oil. Leave for a few hours, and then scrape the label – it should slide off. Eucalyptus essential oil is great for getting glue marks off glass – just dab a cloth with a few drops, and wipe.

removing strong odours

Jars that have previously contained strong-smelling foods such as pickles or chutneys will sometimes retain the smell. A wash in hot soapy water helps remove odours, as can standing the jars and lids in full sun for a few hours (sunlight is also great for removing turmeric stains). Filling your jars with water and adding a teaspoon of sodium bicarbonate (baking soda) and/or placing lids in a bowl of water with sodium bicarbonate and leaving to soak is another option.

It can be more difficult to remove smells from jar lids because they often have a plastic lining which absorbs odours more strongly than glass. If necessary, it is easy to buy replacement lids at kitchen shops. You can keep the old lids for reuse with strong-smelling foods or leftovers where the odour won't negatively affect the taste.

labelling

It's important to label what's in your pantry, fridge or freezer. Unidentified jars of food tend to get thrown away, as do meals made with misidentified ingredients. Mistaking sugar for salt or sodium bicarbonate for rice flour isn't going to end well. It's also useful to label jars with the date you purchased or made something so you can keep track of how long it's been in your kitchen.

With labelling, prioritise ingredients that are difficult to identify by sight, not just for you but for others in your household – flours or spices, for example. Not everyone can tell the difference between ground cumin and ground cinnamon by smell.

I don't use permanent labels because I prefer not to have dedicated jars for different ingredients. I like the flexibility of being able to buy extra of something if I want to make a particular recipe, or decant the contents of an almost empty jar into something smaller to free up space (and the jar). I use a wax pencil to label my jars (sometimes called a chinagraph; you can find them in art supply stores). You could also label with paper tape or washi tape, scrap paper and string, blackboard paint and chalk, or a marker pen, if you have one.

Light can damage food. If any of your containers are continuously exposed to light, it may be better to choose opaque ones. An easy DIY is to paint the outside of glass jars with blackboard paint. Coffee, tea, spices and oils are particularly sensitive to light, as are fortified foods.

reducing food waste:
the pantry

There are a number of reasons that food gets wasted in the pantry – for example it spoils before we can use it, or pests get to it before we do.

Ideally, your pantry is in a cool, dry area of the house, away from the oven and other sources of heat, with doors that block out the light. Avoiding open shelves that get direct sunlight or keeping groceries directly above the stovetop will extend the life of our food. When we don't have the luxury of choice when it comes to food storage spaces, we just need to be more mindful of not overbuying and of using things up more quickly.

The best way to store items in the pantry is in airtight containers. This keeps out air, moisture and pantry pests. As well as helping your food last longer, containers are easier to organise and stack, plus there is less chance of the contents spilling than if you leave things in other packaging.

Some pantry foods will actually keep much better in the fridge or freezer without affecting their taste or texture. If we're limited for space in the fridge or freezer, we can prioritise the most vulnerable or expensive ingredients, and try to buy smaller quantities more often of anything that is susceptible to going bad.

Extend the life of pantry items:

+ **Pantry:** 3 months
+ **Fridge:** 6 months
+ **Freezer:** 1 year +

pantry items to consider storing in the fridge or freezer

Whole, chopped and ground nuts and seeds
(including almond meal, coconut flour, ground flaxseed)

Nut butters

Oils
(oils may go cloudy in the fridge, but will return to normal at room temperature)

Whole grains and wholegrain flours

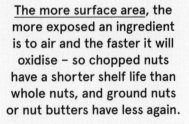

<u>The more surface area</u>, the more exposed an ingredient is to air and the faster it will oxidise – so chopped nuts have a shorter shelf life than whole nuts, and ground nuts or nut butters have less again.

what spoils food in the pantry

Air	Over time, exposure to oxygen causes some food to go bad (oxidation is the main reason for loss of quality in fats, such as when nuts turn rancid). Many bacteria and all moulds require oxygen to grow. Reducing the surface area of food reduces exposure to air and slows down these processes.
Heat	Higher temperatures cause food to break down faster, and can change the appearance and flavour and reduce nutrients. Heat increases the rate of oxidation.
Light	Exposure to light can cause photodegradation, which results in discolouration, reduction in flavour and decline in nutrient content. Fats, proteins, pigments and vitamins are particularly sensitive to light, and liquids are more sensitive than solids (with solids, light can only penetrate the outer surface).
Moisture and humidity	Moisture affects food by allowing bacteria, yeast and mould to grow. This is why dried food keeps better than wet food, and why drying food is used as a method of food preservation. Moisture condensing on the surface of food due to humidity can affect quality – for example, causing soggy cereal or crackers, and making flour clump together.
Smells	Some foods absorb the flavour of other foods, which can affect the taste. Butter, milk, eggs and bread products (including flours and baked goods) are particularly sensitive. Keep sensitive foods away from strong-smelling foods, and ensure jar lids are not tainted.

avoiding pantry pests

No one wants to find pests in their pantry. If we understand what they are and where they come from, we can take steps to prevent them appearing.

The most common offenders are pantry moths, which includes any moths found in the kitchen that feed on grains (such as the Indian meal moth and the Mediterranean flour moth) and weevils, tiny beetles about 2 millimetres in length (the most common types are the granary weevil and the rice weevil). The good news is, they are not harmful, do not carry disease, have nothing to do with cleanliness and do not damage our home – although that doesn't mean we'd choose to eat them.

Moths and weevils can lay their eggs in food in the field, granary or storage facility, long before it reaches our pantry. The eggs are often present in flours and grains, and just as likely to be in pre-packaged products as unpackaged products, although you won't be able to see them: moth eggs are less than 1 millimetre in diameter. They can take several months to hatch and the first thing you'll probably notice is moths in the pantry or beetles in your grains or flour.

Pantry pests and their eggs can be controlled by heating and freezing. If you'd rather not find any surprises in your groceries, get into the habit of freezing grains, flours, nuts and pulses for a period of three days to destroy the eggs before storing in the pantry. (Alternatively, heating to 60 °C/140 °F for fifteen minutes will kill the eggs, but heating isn't appropriate for everything.)

Other pests (like ants and cockroaches) occasionally make their way into the pantry. Ensuring food is stored in airtight containers stops pests getting into food, and helps prevent them spreading.

Always wash your jars with hot soapy water between refills and avoid taking half-filled jars to the bulk store to top up with new ingredients to reduce the risk of pantry pests.

rotating your pantry contents

Every three months or so, it is helpful to take everything out of the pantry to:

+ Check for signs of spoilage or pests
+ Identify any duplicate items
+ Find things we'd forgotten about
+ Discover ingredients that have been in storage for a while and need using up

We can make sure any overstocked items stay off the shopping list for a while and we can look up recipes to ensure we start to use these things up before they go bad. We can also reposition those things that have been in the pantry the longest at the front so we are most likely to use them.

Where a label tells us 'store in a cool place' the ideal room temperature is usually 10 °C (50 °F), which is a lot colder than most of us keep our kitchens. Warmer kitchens will reduce the shelf life of food.

storing fruit and vegetables correctly

As tempting as it is to pile everything in the fridge and hope for the best, learning how to store fresh produce correctly can extend its life considerably, and reduce what we throw away. Some produce stores better on the counter, and some might need to ripen on the counter but then will keep longer in the fridge. We didn't buy these things intending to toss them in the bin, so let's do our best to ensure that doesn't happen!

Many fruit and vegetables release a colourless, odourless gas called ethylene. Ethylene is actually a plant hormone, speeding up ripening of some produce but also negatively affecting other types of produce, causing yellowing or changing the texture. Different fruits and vegetables produce different amounts of ethylene (and some do not produce any at all), and have different sensitivities to it.

As a general rule, fruit produces more ethylene than vegetables, and vegetables are more sensitive to ethylene than fruit. Ideally, it's better to keep high ethylene–producing fruit separate from other fruit, and keep fruit separate from vegetables (in particular broccoli and leafy greens).

guide to ethylene

High ethylene–producing fruits
(store alone)

Apples, ripe avocados, melon (cantaloupe/rockmelon, honeydew), guavas, kiwi fruit, mangoes, papaya, stone fruit, quinces, tomatoes

Ethylene-sensitive vegetables
(store away from ethylene-producing fruit)

Asparagus, unripe avocados, beetroot, brassicas (broccoli, bok choi, cabbage, cauliflower), carrots, celery, cucumber, eggplant/aubergine, lettuce, mushrooms, parsnips, pumpkins/squash

Low to non ethylene–producing/non-sensitive fruits

Berries (blackberries, blueberries, raspberries, strawberries), cherries, figs, citrus (grapefruit, lemons, limes, oranges), lychees, pineapples, pomegranates, rhubarb

Low ethylene–producing/non-sensitive vegetables

Sweetcorn, garlic, ginger, kohlrabi, onions, capsicum/peppers

The produce listed below is usually best kept out of the fridge; for everything else – and any of the following that have been cut – store in the fridge.

+ **Most ethylene-producing fruit, including avocados:** once ripe they can be stored in the fridge
+ **Bananas:** overripe bananas can be frozen
+ **Citrus fruit**
+ **Tomatoes:** ripe tomatoes can be refrigerated to prevent overripening
+ **Potatoes**

+ **Sweet potatoes and yams**
+ **Pumpkins/squash:** some will keep for several months outside the fridge
+ **Garlic:** keep in a dark place to slow down sprouting
+ **Onions:** refrigerating causes the starch to turn to sugar, which makes onions soft and soggy

It's always worth thinking about how seasons might affect your counter produce: remember, the warmer it is, the faster changes (such as ripening, overripening and sprouting) will occur. If you notice fruit or vegetables that are 'supposed' to be kept on the counter becoming overripe, developing black spots or going soft, place in the fridge to slow down the ripening and any decay, and plan to use as soon as possible.

Not only do apples produce a lot of ethylene, they are also sensitive to it. Apples can be kept for a week or two outside the fridge, but will begin to go soft and taste floury. Refrigerated, they are more likely to last 6–8 weeks.

<u>Store potatoes</u> in a dark, dry, cool place.
Light causes potatoes to turn green
and produce solanine, which is toxic
(green potatoes need to be discarded).
Keep potatoes and onions separate, as they
speed up spoilage of one another. Storing
potatoes with an apple can actually help
stop sprouting.

reducing food waste:
the fridge

The ideal fridge temperature is below 5 °C (40 °F), but most fridges are set warmer than this, which means food goes bad more quickly than is necessary. Check the temperature in your fridge using a thermometer. Newer fridges and those that are 'frost-free' tend to circulate air more evenly so there is less variation in temperature than with older models, but even so, fridges aren't the same temperature throughout.

+ The warmest place is the door, so it's best to avoid storing dairy products (including non-dairy equivalents) and other fast-perishing items here.
+ Hot air rises and cold air sinks, so the coolest parts will be the bottom shelves and at the back of the fridge. Meat, poultry and seafood are best kept on the bottom shelf. Partly this is because it is the coldest spot; but also if the packaging leaks they will not drip onto other foods.

To keep your fridge cold, try to avoid opening the fridge door for too long – all the warm air in the room will get inside and it will take a while to cool back down again. Also, make sure that cooked foods have cooled down before placing in the fridge. A worn fridge door seal will increase the temperature and cost more to run, so if you notice gaps or draughts, invest in a replacement seal.

It's useful to keep a tray or a shelf in the fridge for food that needs using up as a priority – ideally labelled 'eat me first'. If there are other people in your household, encourage them to check and take from this spot before eating anything else in the fridge.

the crisper

In the main part of the fridge, moisture from food diffuses into the air or gets sucked into the fan. That's why food seems to dry out or go limp in the fridge; inside crisper drawers, however, moisture is trapped. If you have a single crisper drawer, the best thing to store here is thin-skinned fruit and vegetables, such as leafy greens and berries. If you have two crisper drawers, you can use one for vegetables and the other for fruit.

Some crisper drawers have a vent. If you're trying to keep humidity in and stop your veggies going limp, keep this vent closed. If you are storing ethylene-producing fruit, keeping the vent closed will encourage them to ripen, so you may prefer to keep it open.

If you're limited for space in your fridge, you can store leafy greens and herbs for a week or two at room temperature in a glass of water, as you might flowers in a vase. Cut the tips of the stems off first, and change the water every day or so. Remove any leaves or stems that become slimy.

fridge storage without plastic wrap

The common wisdom is to wrap things in plastic so they keep better in the fridge. We're trying to use less single-use plastic and ditch the clingfilm, but we don't want things going bad sooner as a result. Here's what you can use instead.

Reusable wax wraps

These are pieces of cotton that have been coated with wax (usually beeswax and jojoba, but wholly plant-based wax versions are also available), which makes them waterproof but breathable. They also contain tree rosin (usually damar or pine rosin, sometimes called colophony), which makes them sticky and more adhesive. Wax wraps are useful for wrapping cheese and cut produce, and covering bowls and plates.

Storage containers with lids

Any lidded container is going to create a high-humidity environment and reduce wilting. They're also going to trap strong smells. Glass jars and old plastic containers and lunch boxes you already have will do the trick, while rectangular glass storage containers are a good investment (I choose oven-safe glass so my containers can double up as oven dishes).

A damp tea towel

Leafy greens or anything that tends to go limp in the fridge can be loosely wrapped in a damp (but not soaking wet) tea towel.

Silicone storage bags/ sandwich pockets

Reusable food storage bags take up far less space in the fridge (and freezer) than rigid containers. They are also more versatile than plastic: the best ones are completely leakproof, microwave and dishwasher safe and can withstand temperatures up to 200 °C (400 °F). Silicone storage bags are not cheap, but with proper care will last a lifetime.

A plate over a bowl/ bowl over a plate

Simply placing a plate over a bowl of leftovers or prepared produce will help reduce moisture loss. It won't be airtight, but close enough, and food will keep better than if uncovered.

Silicone lids (stretchy and non stretchy)

A reusable alternative to the plate/bowl method that provides a better seal.

If you already have reusable plastic containers, don't feel any pressure to get rid of them and invest in 'better' alternatives. It's always going to be less wasteful to use what we already have. If you're concerned about reusing your plastic containers for food storage, repurpose them to other areas of the house.

reducing food waste:
the freezer

Freezers are great for extending the life of our food. They also change the texture of some foods, particularly fresh fruits and vegetables; the water content expands when frozen, which breaks the plant cell walls and makes them mushy. This is fine if they will be cooked or used in baking. It's often easier to add part-frozen fruit or vegetables directly to whatever you're cooking rather than allowing to thaw first.

The other change that can negatively affect our food is freezer burn. This is discolouration and other damage caused by the moisture in the outer layers of the food evaporating into the freezer air, which leaves behind empty 'dry' pockets in the food. Freezer burn is usually visible as puckered white splotches, or on meat as brown-white discolouration. It isn't harmful, but it does affect flavour and texture, and it can't be reversed.

To keep freezer burn to a minimum, pack food as tightly as possible to reduce exposure to the air, and seal containers properly once frozen. Ensure you don't put anything into the freezer while still hot, and ideally chill food before freezing. This slows freezer burn down but it won't prevent it forever, so aim to eat the oldest food in the freezer first.

tips for freezing

Cooked vegetables

Because cooked vegetables have lost moisture during the cooking process, they are less affected by freezing. Leftover roasted vegetables, soups, stews and sauces freeze particularly well.

Raw vegetables

Raw vegetables freeze best if they are blanched first: put them into a pan of boiling water for a minute or so (the time varies depending on the size and type of vegetables), transfer to a bowl of icy water, drain thoroughly, then freeze. Blanching helps retain crunch and colour, and kills bugs. It also wilts some vegetables so that they take up less space in the freezer.

Fruit

Freezing fruit in large containers tends to mean everything clumps together, and it's impossible to separate without defrosting the whole container. Instead, lay fruit slices or berries (or other foods you'd like to be able to separate) on a tray in the freezer, and once frozen place in a container. Some fruits (stone fruit, apples) brown when exposed to air and when frozen. If this bothers you, dipping in lemon juice before freezing will help reduce browning.

Bread

Bread freezes better when wrapped, and the longer you intend to store it, the more it needs wrapping. If you're freezing for more than a few days, a moisture-proof cover is recommended: wax wraps work well, or you can purchase a double-layer recycled plastic bread bag specifically designed for freezing (I recommend Onya bread bags).

Meat and fish

With meat and fish, store in a sealed container. If you intend to freeze for an extended period, wrap the portions in parchment paper and then in foil, before sealing in the container.

freezer storage

Freezing food in plastic is often suggested because it's easy to squeeze all the air out, it takes up less space than containers and it's easy to pack into the freezer. The questions to ask are: how much space do we have, how much are we trying to store and how long do we intend to freeze it for? Homesteaders trying to preserve an entire harvest or a year's worth of produce have very different needs to someone who just cooked too much sweet potato this week.

If you're really limited for freezer space, consider investing in some reusable silicone storage bags (I recommend Stasher bags). They take up less space than containers, and as you remove food from them you can squeeze the air out, which helps protect your still-frozen food and frees up space. A cheaper but bulkier option is to freeze in glass jars and glass containers.

Some glass brands, such as Pyrex, or canning jars like Ball Mason, Weck, Kilner or Fowlers Vacola, are officially deemed 'freezer safe'. However, with a bit of care it's possible to freeze in other glass jars, too. I look for round jars with thick glass and straight sides or that taper outwards; jam jars are ideal. Avoid any with narrow necks or that taper inwards, like sauce bottles; food expands when freezing and if there's no room for this expansion, the jar will crack.

When you fill the jar, fill to the widest point, and if the jar has shoulders, do not fill right to the top of the curve. The more water something contains, the more it will expand. Ensure the food is chilled before placing in the freezer, and leave the jar lid off in case the contents expand. Once frozen, screw the lid on tightly and label your jar.

<u>There is such a thing as a free lunch, and it's leftovers!</u> I love leftovers so much that I always cook at least twice as much as I need for a meal. The initial chopping and prepping might take a little longer when making more, but the cooking time remains pretty constant, as does the amount of washing up. Intentionally creating leftovers is planning for future us: there is nothing better after a long day of work or a busy weekend than to find a prepared meal waiting in the fridge or freezer.

Whether you deliberately created leftovers or you just cooked more than you can eat, it's all good news. If you think you will eat them within the following week, pop them in a suitable lidded container in the fridge as soon as they've cooled down. Otherwise, pop in the freezer.

what's all the fuss about: composting

Inevitably, some of the food we buy needs to be tossed. Food eventually goes bad. Leftovers sometimes go uneaten. Most fruit and vegetables have inedible bits: pips, seeds, rinds and cores. Rather than putting it in the landfill bin, we can do something better with these scraps.

Composting is the breaking down of organic material by bacteria, fungi, worms and insects in the presence of air (specifically, oxygen) to create compost, a rich organic matter that can be added to soil to increase carbon and support plant growth.

Many people mistakenly believe that landfills are like big composting piles, but they are not like compost bins at all. Landfills are designed to ensure composting does *not* happen. When waste arrives at a landfill site, it is deposited in 'cells'. Cells are engineered depressions in the ground that take months to construct, and are lined with plastics, clay and rocks to prevent liquid waste leaching into groundwater and the soil. The landfill waste is compacted to maximise space and increase stability, and then covered with a layer of plastic or rocks to exclude oxygen. In these conditions, food breaks down very slowly, releasing methane (a potent greenhouse gas) and carbon dioxide. It can take thirty years for a landfill cell to release all the methane. Methane is also flammable and poses a fire risk long after the cells are filled.

In composting speak, 'organic' means anything that was once alive. From a chemistry perspective it means 'containing carbon' – and all living or once-living things contain carbon. This is different to 'organic food', which refers to the growing of food without synthetic chemicals.

In Australia, 87 per cent of food waste currently goes to landfill. Landfills are the third-largest source of human-related methane emissions in the USA, accounting for more than 14 per cent of emissions. Not only do they generate greenhouse gases, they also waste valuable nutrients. Composting, on the other hand, recycles those nutrients and improves soil health.

Ensuring our food waste is composted makes a huge dent in what we send to landfill. As well as saving nutrients and reducing greenhouse gases it means less land wasted, less energy used and fewer trucks on the road (landfills and cities don't mix, and many landfills are located far from where the densely populated areas are).

systems for food scraps

In-ground compost

For those with a backyard, it's straightforward to set up a basic compost bin that is placed on the ground (ideally digging in the base a little to keep things contained). Compost bins require very little maintenance, and provide free compost to use on house plants or on the garden.

Rotary composter

Sometimes called a compost tumbler, this is a fully sealed cylindrical drum mounted on a frame that can be rotated to turn the compost and keep the air moving. Ideal for anyone limited to a patio or balcony, limited for space, or who finds an in-ground compost bin more physically challenging.

Neighbourhood composting hubs

Not everyone has the space, time, capacity or inclination to set up their own food waste composting systems, and some choose instead to make use of neighbourhood composting hubs. Informal options include dropping off food scraps at a local farmers' market or community garden. Some people use the online compost-sharing network ShareWaste to find local composting hubs or people in their area who are happy to accept food scraps for composting. Some councils may also offer a food scrap collection service. Alternatively, there are businesses that will collect food scraps for a fee.

Worm farm

For those living in apartments, worm farms can be more practical than compost bins and are very popular. Worm farms are compact units that use a particular type of worm to break down food (vermicomposting is the technical name). Worm castings (the soil-like substance you get when the worms have munched through the food scraps) are much finer than compost and very nutrient rich. These are great for seedlings, house plants or adding to the garden. Worm farms can be kept outdoors all year round in warm climates (the worms can die if temperatures drop below 5 °C/44 °F).

Bokashi system

Technically not composting, these systems use fermentation and are great for indoor spaces because the contents are kept in a sealed bucket (the process is anaerobic, meaning without oxygen, unlike composting and vermicomposting). Bokashi buckets can be used to deal with meat, fish and cooked food scraps, which are not recommended for compost bins or worm farms. The fermented bokashi bin contents eventually need to be dug into the ground or added to a compost bin, so the system is not suitable for everybody.

composting tips

If you're keen to compost at home, the best site for your compost bin is out of full sun and with easy access to the kitchen. It might seem like a great idea to locate it as far away from the house as possible, but if it's dark and raining outside, are you really going to traipse across the garden to use it?

Compost bins need balance to work properly: a mixture of carbon, nitrogen, air and moisture. All organic matter contains both carbon and nitrogen, but in different ratios. Materials high in carbon are often called 'brown' because they are dry; materials high in nitrogen are often called 'green' because they are fresh, moist and usually green in colour (all food scraps are classed as 'green'). Too much carbon and the compost will decompose very slowly; too much nitrogen and the compost will begin to smell (this is the most common mistake people make with home composting).

Do compost at home:

+ All fruit and vegetables, including peels and pips
+ Cotton, tissues and kitchen towel
+ Vacuum cleaner dust
+ Feathers, fur and hair
+ Small amounts of leftovers
+ Soiled bedding from vegetarian animals (rabbits, guinea pigs, hamsters)

To balance the carbon and nitrogen and avoid a stinky compost bin, we need two parts brown and one part green. In simple terms: for every handful of food scraps that we add to the compost bin, we need to add two handfuls of 'brown'. Dry leaves, shredded paper, sawdust, egg cartons and cardboard are all 'brown' and carbon rich. Keeping a box of these materials next to the compost is the easiest way to get the balance right.

Your compost should smell earthy, and be moist to touch but not dripping wet. Composting is a living system, needing living organisms to break down the waste. As well as bacteria there will be worms, insects and other critters living in your compost bin. Don't be put off by this: they all have a role to play.

It's also helpful to layer your compost. If you have a lot of food scraps, add some, add the brown layer, add more food scraps and continue to create multiple thin layers. It's best to finish with a brown layer to cover the food and reduce the likelihood of insects laying eggs, and reduce flies.

Turning your compost will increase oxygen flow and help food scraps break down faster. You can buy compost forks (which look like giant corkscrews) to assist with turning the compost. A pitchfork will also do the job, or you might prefer to set up a rotary compost bin. Turning your compost every week is ideal.

Adding meat, fish and large amounts of dairy to a compost bin attracts vermin and encourages flies (and maggots). Instead, process these with a bokashi bin, and once fermented, add to the compost bin.

Troubleshooting common composting problems:

+ **Too dry** (looks and feels dry, ants are present): add moisture.
+ **Too wet** (contents are sodden): turn compost, and add dry carbon materials such as cardboard, paper or dry leaves.
+ **Vermin:** ensure bin is dug into the ground, consider using mouse mesh at the base.
+ **Flies:** turn compost, ensure food is buried and cover top with a layer of soil.
+ **Smelly:** turn compost, add dry ingredients such as cardboard, paper or dry leaves.
+ **Not doing anything:** ensure contents are moist, ensure there is enough nitrogen-rich (green) material, boost with a few handfuls of fresh compost, manure or composting worms.

part five

getting started in your (less waste no fuss) kitchen

kitting out your kitchen

Reducing waste – and fuss! – in the kitchen is not just about the food in our pantries and fridges; what we use to prepare that food matters too. Whether you love cooking or simply want the job done as quickly as possible, kitchen equipment that saves resources, time and money is always going to win. It is amazing what a difference it makes to set up your kitchen as thoughtfully as your pantry.

useful kitchen tools

For a kitchen tool or gadget to be truly useful (and not just taking up space in a cupboard or drawer somewhere) it needs to save us time and do the job at least as well as *and preferably better* than we'd manage without it. It needs to be easily accessible when we want to use it, easy to use and easy to clean afterwards.

Tools are there to make life easier, not harder.

There are so many kitchen gadgets and tools out there, and one person's 'essential' is another person's 'waste of money'. As a rule, it is better to have a few tools you use often rather than a lot that rarely get touched, require constant cupboard rearranging and create a cluttered, chaotic kitchen that lends itself to ordering takeaway rather than actually cooking.

I keep things low waste and no fuss with a few key kitchen items. Where possible I'd always choose glass or stainless steel over plastic because these materials don't stain or scratch as easily, can handle heat and are much easier to clean.

Before investing in an item, read reviews of models online and think about what features you need and would actually use. Second-hand gadgets are a great way to save some money and test something out – if you don't get on with it, it should be easy to sell again.

Knife

There is one tool that absolutely every kitchen needs, and that is a good, *sharp* knife. Think about it. We use a knife every single time we prepare food. Why wouldn't we invest in the best one we can afford? We think nothing of spending money on food processors, bread machines, ice cream makers and other gadgets that we might use only a few times a month. Yet for the one tool we use most often, we purchase something cheap and then lament our choice two weeks later when we realise that it can't cut cleanly through an avocado.

A good knife is a buy-it-once purchase (look after it and it will last you your whole life) and worth every penny.

I own two kitchen knives: a bread knife with a serrated edge for cutting bread and, for everything else, a Global vegetable knife with a 14-centimetre (5½-inch) blade. It's the perfect size blade and handle for me, made from one piece of stainless steel, meaning the handle can never fall off, and it can be sharpened with a sharpening stone or taken to a knife sharpener for servicing. I've owned that knife for more than fifteen years, and it will last forever.

Are dishwashers eco-friendly? I don't think the answer is a simple yes or no. From a water perspective, modern dishwashers are actually more water efficient than washing dishes by hand. From an energy perspective, making a dishwasher from metals and plastic has a higher footprint than the sink we already have in the kitchen. But it's not just about footprints. If a dishwasher is what you need to maintain order in the kitchen, then embrace it. If you can manage without, embrace your sink. Whichever we choose, we can still be mindful of the resources we use – whether that's power, water or the detergent we choose.

my kitchen essentials

Measuring cups

A simple way to measure basic ingredients such as flour and sugar. US and Australian recipes often refer to cup measurements rather than weight, and owning a set of these is less fuss than trying to convert a recipe.

Kitchen scales

The most accurate way to measure ingredients is with kitchen scales. When choosing scales you have the option of balance, mechanical or battery-operated. It's worth considering how much accuracy you need, whether you'd prefer metric or imperial measurements or both, and also the maximum load you'll want to weigh. I have electric scales that can measure to the nearest gram or 0.1 ounce and take up to 5 kilograms (11 pounds).

Measuring jug

Useful for measuring and pouring larger volumes of liquids (such as when adding stock to a saucepan). A measuring jug is great for figuring out the volume of glass jars (for bulk store shopping). I use a glass Pyrex jug that holds 500 ml (1 pint), with metric measurements printed on one side in 50 ml increments, and imperial and cup measurements in ¼ cup increments printed on the other.

Pestle and mortar

Useful for grinding up spices and seeds, and making pastes and dips.

Silicone spatula

I use this all the time. It is perfect for getting every last drop of sauce, batter or leftovers out of a bowl or pan, and silicone is tolerant of high temperatures (unlike plastic).

Food processor/blender

If I had to choose just one gadget, I'd always vote for a high-power food processor or blender. Mine saves me so much time chopping, grinding and blending. I'd recommend choosing one that's easy to take apart and wash.

rethinking single-use items in the kitchen

There are a number of single-use items we come to rely on in the kitchen. Reusable items are often an 'investment' – meaning they cost a lot upfront, but will last and save you money in the long run. That being said, there are definitely options for every budget. Stepping back and looking at our waste can lead us to question whether we actually need these things at all. Could we do without or switch to a reusable alternative?

Single use: just because the manufacturer labels something single use, that doesn't mean we need to limit it to one use. Aluminium foil can be washed and reused several times, as can ziplock bags and other plastic. Baking paper can often be wiped down and reused a few times before composting.

Clingfilm/ plastic wrap	From placing a plate on a bowl to switching to reusable silicone, there is a reusable solution for every need you might have thought you had for plastic wrap (see page 126 for some ideas).
Paper towel/ kitchen roll	Consider using a dishcloth for wiping spills, or using old tea towels to absorb excess liquids and then washing before reusing. It's possible to buy purpose-made 'unpaper towel': reusable fabric cut to size, often attached to form a roll.
Bin liners	If you still buy food in packaging, could any of that packaging be used as a bin liner? Could you line your bin with old newspaper? Could you do away with a liner altogether?
Baking paper/ parchment paper	Some brands of paper have a thin layer of plastic and may be bleached with chlorine. A reusable alternative is silicone baking sheets. If you prefer baking paper, If You Care are a brand making Forest Stewardship Council–certified compostable baking paper. Choose a roll rather than pre-cut sheets to reduce the waste.
Aluminium foil	If you use foil for wrapping leftovers, consider switching to a reusable alternative. If you use it in cooking, look for a brand that is 100 per cent recycled.
Muffin cases	A thorough greasing of baking tins can reduce the need for single-use muffin cases. Alternatively, silicone bakeware is oven safe and reusable. If sticking with single-use, choose unbleached paper and avoid glitter or metallic papers that are not compostable.
Ziplock bags	Reusable silicone storage bags are much sturdier and long lasting – plus the best ones are oven, microwave and dishwasher safe.
Wooden skewers	A fun alternative is to use rosemary sprigs: remove the leaves and use the central stem. Metal skewers have the advantage of reducing cooking time (hot metal cooks the inside of the food).
Plastic straws	Consider reusable bamboo, glass, stainless steel and coloured metal or silicone options: almost all are dishwasher safe.

better food, full stop

Using less packaging means buying more foods that *are* ingredients, rather than food products made from ingredients. When I first decided to reduce my waste in the kitchen, I had no intention of changing the things I bought, only the way I bought them. However, I began to notice that some things were easier to buy packaging-free than others, some were more affordable than others, and some were available locally grown. A lot of the ingredients I buy now I had never heard of when I started out – and I definitely didn't know how to cook them!

I didn't consider my previous diet to be unhealthy. But by avoiding packaging, I realised how much 'convenience' food I had been buying (empty calories that just drained my wallet and created packaging waste). Rather than buying processed junk food, I started buying more fresh fruit and vegetables, and whole foods.

For me, unprocessed, unpackaged, local and natural came hand in hand with a healthier diet. There are plenty of food pyramids and 'meal plates', but the Healthy Eating Plate created by nutrition experts at the Harvard School of Public Health really reflects this way of eating. It's a great model: it's simple, focuses on food groups rather than specific products, and gives guidelines rather than instructions. It was developed to address what the creators saw as deficiencies in government-produced healthy eating guidelines, which mix science with the influence of powerful agricultural interests. While different diets work for different people, these principles of choosing more fresh, whole and natural foods are something we lean towards as we start to reduce waste in the kitchen. As you choose your ingredients and plan your meals, you might find it helpful to keep this model in mind.

Illustration adapted from the Harvard School of Public Health Healthy Eating Plate. This diagram is for informational purposes. It is not intended to offer personal medical advice. Seek the advice of your physician or other qualified health provider with any questions you may have regarding any medical conditions.

Healthy plant oils

In moderation

Whole grains

¼ of the plate

Vegetables and fruits

½ of the plate
(potatoes don't count)

Protein

¼ of the plate (limit red meat and avoid processed meats such as bacon)

recipes are made to be broken

I'm not sure I've ever met a recipe I haven't tweaked in some way. From substituting ingredients because I don't have those suggested, to making my own 'improvements' (leaving out things I don't like, adding extra of things I do), to omitting steps just to keep things simpler and less fuss, I rarely stick to a recipe and it always works out.

It's not that I'm a gifted cook. I wish! It's more that there is only so much space in my pantry for ingredients, I rarely check recipes until after the shops close and I'm a master of making do.

Chefs have had years of training; it is their job to make amazing creations and finesse their recipes. But I'm not trying to recreate restaurant-quality meals. I just want the job done. I've had years of needing to make dinner every evening after work, and my priority is to make something quick and simple with what I have to hand. Plus, my preferences are unique to me. A chef might think that caraway seeds 'make' a recipe, or a cake really needs two cups of sugar, but my tastebuds often disagree.

Confidence in the kitchen is not something we're born with; it is something we learn. When I first left home at eighteen, I literally did not know how to boil pasta. But when you eat food three times a day, every day, you gradually get more familiar with different ingredients, learn different techniques and grow your confidence. Nowadays, I consider it my superpower to be able to create a meal out of fridge 'dregs', or rustle something together even when there's 'nothing in the fridge'. It's a matter of practice, and that comes with time.

Don't be afraid to change ingredients and make swaps when cooking with a recipe. It's all valuable practice – and if an ingredient is particularly important to a dish, or if there's a step that's critical for success, the recipe will tell you, so you'll know not to switch these things out. Other times, the recipe might tell you what characteristics the ingredients have, which can help with substitution. For example, if a recipe mentions that the almonds add crunch, they could probably be switched out for most other nuts or seeds, or even something like croutons. If you're nervous about switching an entire ingredient, try switching out half instead.

Generally, like can be swapped for like. Meaning, most protein can be switched out for other protein, grains for other grains, nuts or seeds for other nuts and seeds, and so on. The tuna in a salad can be switched for chickpeas, risotto can be made with wheat berries or buckwheat, porridge can be made with quinoa or millet, peanut butter can be switched for almond butter, pine nuts for chopped cashew pieces, dried cherries for dried cranberries, and so it goes on. Over time, we learn our favourites and when we see a recipe that uses something else, we switch in what we have.

If you're new to bulk shopping or experimenting with cooking vegetarian meals for the first time, don't be worried by all the varieties and strange names or wonder what on earth you might do with these things! We'll introduce some of them shortly, and in time you can explore whether they are something you'd like to add (or swap) into your diet.

no fuss swaps

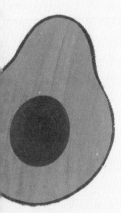

Fat

Avocados, coconut, nuts, seeds
and oils are all high in fat. They can
replace dairy in recipes (such as
sprinkling toasted nuts over a salad
in place of cheese), or one type
can be switched for another.

Sugar

Sugar is an ingredient in its
own right, but many foods add
sweetness to recipes: dates in
particular, most fresh and dried
fruit, tomatoes and coconut flakes
(which are sometimes sweetened,
but even unsweetened coconut
has a sweet flavour).

Salt

As well as salt, brined foods
(such as olives), soy sauce, tamari
and miso all add saltiness.

Acid/sour

Vinegars, lemon, lime and grapefruit juice, preserved lemons, pickled vegetables (preserved in vinegar), capers, fermented vegetables and dried sour cherries all add acidic or sour notes to a dish.

Freshness

Having a raw, uncooked component to a meal adds something extra. It could be flavour, crunch or simply colour. Try fresh herbs (basil, coriander/cilantro, flat-leaf/Italian parsley and mint are all great added to dishes upon serving), fresh greens, spring onions, bean sprouts, or a few strips of fresh lemon or orange zest (for both savoury and sweet dishes).

know your herbs and spices

Herbs and spices add lots of flavour to a meal, but there are so many varieties our pantry can end up overwhelmed with things we never use (and that go to waste). Recipes always seem to 'need' spices that we don't have. Rather than owning every spice that ever existed, I prefer to choose a few with distinct flavours that are my regulars, and use these in place of ones I don't have when following a recipe. Cumin, coriander, cinnamon, turmeric and smoked paprika are all staples in my pantry, and I rotate a few others to keep things interesting.

If you see a spice or herb in a recipe that you don't have, ask the internet if there's a suitable swap. Mace is related to nutmeg; caraway seeds are related to cumin, anise and dill seeds; chilli powder, hot paprika and cayenne pepper will all give a hot kick to a dish.

Some spices are actually a mix of other spices we already have. If you don't cook often, you may prefer to buy the ready-mixed blends. On the other hand, if you already have plenty of spices in your pantry, you may prefer making your own versions of these blends from spices you have, to avoid doubling up.

If you have a spice grinder or pestle and mortar, you could buy only whole spices (rather than buying the whole and the ground version) and grind as you need. It helps keep pantry clutter down and reduces the likelihood of spices going stale, and freshly ground spices always taste better than pre-ground versions.

make your own spice mixes

Chilli powder
There are two types of chilli powder: one is 100 per cent ground chillies, the other is a mix used to season chilli (the Mexican dish). The mix usually contains chilli powder along with cumin, oregano and powdered onion and/or garlic.

Chinese five spice
Star anise, cinnamon, fennel seeds, black pepper and cloves.

Curry powder
Ingredients vary, but usually include turmeric, coriander and cumin, with variations of other spices including fennel, mustard powder, ginger and powdered onion and/or garlic (cayenne pepper or chilli will be in the hotter versions).

Garam masala
A fragrant blend of coriander, cinnamon and cloves; other spices vary, including black pepper, cumin, turmeric, ginger, cardamom, nutmeg, fennel and/or dill seeds.

Italian seasoning
The main ingredient is usually marjoram or oregano, with other ingredients varying, including rosemary, thyme, basil, sage and powdered onion and/or garlic.

Mixed spice
Ingredients vary, with coriander, cinnamon and nutmeg most common; ginger, cloves, allspice and/or caraway are sometimes included.

Za'atar
Sesame seeds, sumac, dried oregano, cumin and salt.

know your sugars

Unless you're a professional pastry chef, you don't need fifteen types of sugar in your pantry. Knowing which varieties are most similar can help you choose the best swaps, keeping packaging and pantry clutter down, and reducing food waste. Find some staples you like, and stick with those.

As a general rule, the darker a sugar is, the more molasses (and minerals) it retains. To keep flavours similar, keep colour similar (light-coloured sugars have a more subtle flavour; darker ones have more intensity); however, don't be afraid to experiment. Solids and liquids can be switched too, but you'll need to either adjust the dry elements if using a liquid, or add another (or more) liquid if using dry sugar.

solid sugars

Refined

Granulated, caster, superfine and icing are actually the same type of highly refined sugar, just with incrementally smaller crystals (icing/confectioners' sugar is a powder). It's possible to make the others from granulated sugar using a blender, grinder or pestle and mortar – first you will get caster, then superfine; continue grinding to make icing sugar. Golden sugar (called raw sugar in Australia) is simply refined white sugar with a tiny amount of molasses added back in to make it golden. 'Brown' sugar is actually white granulated sugar with molasses added back in. It's easy to make your own: add 1 spoon of molasses for every 6 spoons of sugar to make light brown sugar, and 1 spoon of molasses for every 3 spoons of sugar to make dark brown sugar.

Less refined

Turbinado and demerara sugars are semi-processed brown sugars. Muscovado sugar is less processed again: it retains its molasses during processing and looks almost identical to dark brown sugar. Other less processed options include rapadura, panela, jaggery, palm and coconut sugars, which can also be used instead of brown sugar.

liquid sugars

Maple syrup

Made from the sap of the maple tree, this sweetener can vary in colour from golden to dark (the darker varieties have a stronger flavour) and is only produced in Canada and the USA. Maple-flavoured syrup is often made from corn syrup or cane sugar, artificial colour and flavouring, and preservatives.

Honey

Made by bees using the nectar of flowering plants (different plants impart different flavours and colours). It is usually possible to find a local option. Honey is not considered vegan.

Rice malt syrup (sometimes called brown rice syrup), **coconut nectar and agave syrup**

These sweeteners are not made from cane sugar. They are all similar in appearance, with a mild flavour. Agave has light and dark versions; the light one is mild and the darker one has a more intense flavour.

Molasses

Golden syrup (sometimes called light treacle) has a mild flavour and golden colour; black treacle (black molasses) is thicker and darker, more mineral rich, and has a much stronger flavour.

Jam or preserving sugar is white granulated sugar with added pectin and/or citric acid to help jam set. Use regular white sugar and add grated citrus peel (or you can also buy sachets of powdered pectin) to help set preserves.

know your flours

Flours can be trickier than sugars to substitute in recipes, particularly when baking. Different flours have differing amounts of gluten (and some are gluten free), and gluten is what gives baked goods their structure. It influences how much and how well bread and fluffy sponge cakes will rise. For cookies and pancakes, it's less important, and for sauces (where flours are just added to thicken) it shouldn't matter too much.

White flour is wheat flour, wholegrain flour contains more bran, and Italian flour, pasta flour and 0 or 00 flours are finer than white flour. The finer flours might be recommended for pasta or bread making, but white flour will do the job.

One flour, three names

The three most common flours you'll see in baking recipes are plain flour, all-purpose flour and self-raising flour. Plain flour and all-purpose flour are the same thing, a soft wheat flour (it's called plain flour in UK and Australian recipes, and all-purpose in American recipes). Self-raising flour is the same flour except baking powder has been added. Rather than keep both plain and self-raising flour in the pantry, you can keep just plain flour, and add baking powder as needed: 1 teaspoon of baking powder for every 75 grams (2¾ ounces /½ cup) plain flour.

Gluten-free flour isn't actually a single type of flour; it's a term applied to flours made from ingredients that do not contain gluten. Because they vary so much, the same recipe made with two different gluten-free flours may have very different results. I find I get the best results when I follow recipes that specify quantities and types of the different gluten-free flours. Avoid swapping gluten flours for gluten-free flours unless you're a more experienced cook; you're better off looking for recipes designed with gluten-free flours in mind.

Baking powder is just a mix of two
ingredients. To make your own, combine
2 tablespoons of cream of tartar with
1 tablespoon sodium bicarbonate (baking
soda). Commercial baking powders can also
contain cornstarch (a flour actually made
from wheat, containing gluten) and some
have aluminium salts to stop clumping.

know your grains
(and pseudo-grains)

Used to eating mostly white rice and pasta? You're in for a treat! There are many more delicious options that are easy to prepare and switch in to your meals.

Grains, sometimes referred to as cereals, are the seeds of edible grasses. Grains have three parts, from the outside in: the bran, the germ and the endosperm.

Refined grains — Have the bran and germ removed and retain only the endosperm. This gives them a finer texture, improves their shelf life and reduces cooking time, but also removes some of the nutrients, and most (or all) of the fibre.

Whole grains — Have all three parts still intact. Grains also have a tough inedible outer layer called the hull, which is always removed – so hulled grains are still whole grains.

Ancient grains — Can be either true or pseudo-grains; they've changed minimally in the thousands of years they've been grown, unlike modern grains such as wheat, rice and corn, which have been bred selectively.

Pseudo-grains (sometimes called pseudo-cereals) — Are not actually grains but seeds from other plant species. They are prepared and used in similar ways to 'true' grains. All pseudo-grains are naturally gluten free.

<u>Soaking grains</u>: Many grains benefit from soaking; it's not required, but reduces cooking time and improves digestibility. As a general rule, soaking for 8 hours reduces cooking time by 10 minutes.

To soak grains, place in a pan and cover with water, then agitate with your hand to release any dust, starch and grit. Drain and repeat until the water runs clear. Replace the grains in the pan, cover with water, add a squeeze of lemon juice or splash of apple cider vinegar, and leave on the bench at room temperature. Ideally, soak for a few hours (or up to 24 hours): soaking in the morning and cooking in the evening is ideal, or soaking in the evening and cooking for breakfast. When you're ready to go, drain, rinse and cook.

guide to grains

Fuss level +
Pre-cooked grains or those with cooking time 15 minutes or less

Fuss level + +
Cooking time 15–30 minutes

Fuss level + + +
Cooking time 30–60 minutes

Buckwheat
(sometimes called buckwheat groats)

+

Small pyramid-shaped seeds with a strong, almost bitter flavour. Despite the name, buckwheat is not a wheat so it's gluten free. Try buckwheat instead of rice to make risotto.

Bulgur wheat
(sometimes called bourghul)

+

Whole wheat grains that have been parboiled and dried. Cracked bulgur wheat has been crushed into small pieces. Bulgur wheat only requires soaking in boiling water until softened. It is used to make tabouleh salad: let ½ cup bulgur wheat sit for 20 minutes with 3 chopped tomatoes and the juice from half a lemon, then add 3 handfuls of flat-leaf/Italian parsley and a glug of olive oil.

Rolled oats

+

Oat grains that have been steamed and rolled. The thinner the oat, the quicker the cooking time. Instant oats are the thinnest and pre-cooked, perfect for no fuss porridge: add hot water and wait 2 minutes. Rolled oats are great in overnight oats: put ⅓ cup oats and ⅔ cup milk in a jar, add a tablespoon of nut butter, any spices, nuts or dried fruit that you fancy, stir, pop in the fridge and eat the following morning!

Couscous

+

Technically not a grain, these tiny spheres are made from steamed semolina flour (bran and germ removed). Regular couscous is 'instant' and just needs to soak briefly in boiling water; pearl (giant) couscous is a larger version that needs to be boiled. Traditionally served with a tagine, a delicious North African spiced stew.

Cracked freekeh and cracked wheat

+ +

Whole wheat grains that have been crushed into small pieces (and therefore cook faster). Freekeh is a type of wheat grain harvested before fully ripened and burned to remove the chaff, which leaves a smoky flavour.

Quinoa

+

A small round seed that's similar in size to couscous and gluten free. White, red and black quinoa are all grown commercially. When cooked it has a fluffy, light texture and mild flavour. A simple substitute for rice with curries and dal.

Millet

+ +

Refers to a number of different gluten-free cereal crops with small round (usually pale or golden) seeds, resembling couscous. Millet absorbs flavours well and is good for soaking up sauces. It also makes great porridge: cook 1 cup millet with 3 cups liquid (I use the coconut water from page 185) until all the liquid is absorbed, stir through some milk (or coconut cream), and top with nuts, fruit or seeds.

guide to grains

Cornmeal
(medium-grind cornmeal
sometimes labelled polenta)
+ +

Yellow or white dent corn (bran
and germ removed) ground into
a coarse powder. Stone-ground
cornmeal is made from whole
grains and is less common.
Cornmeal has a subtle, nutty
flavour and when cooked, can be
substituted for rice or mashed
potato, or baked and sliced.

Short-grain rice
(white)
+ +

Short, fat grains that are very
starchy and become sticky when
cooked. Varieties include arborio
and carnaroli (used in risotto),
pudding, sushi and paella rice.
Short-grain rice takes longer to
cook than long-grain rice.

Long-grain rice
(white and brown)
+ +

Slender, long grains that contain
less starch than short-grain rice,
so when cooked remain drier and
stay separate. Brown long-grain
rice is wholegrain; white rice has
had the germ and bran removed
and cooks faster. To make cooked
rice more interesting, I often mix
it with the same amount of cooked
Puy lentils or quinoa, and add
a big handful of chopped fresh
herbs (try mint, parsley, basil or
coriander/cilantro).

Freekeh and wheat grain
(often called wheat berries)
+ + +

Whole grains that look like brown
rice, with a nutty flavour and
chewy texture. Both are great
for salads: simply cook and stir
through nuts, herbs, dried or fresh
fruit, vegetables and protein.

Rye
(sometimes called rye berries)

+ + +

A darker brown grain than wheat, with a green hue. It has a slightly sour flavour.

Sorghum
(sometimes called great millet)

+ + +

A rounded seed larger than millet, ranging from white to golden or light brown in colour depending on the variety. A gluten-free grain.

Pearl (pearled) barley

+ + +

Whole grains similar in size to wheat or rye but a paler colour. The outer surface is polished (pearled) to remove some or all of the bran, making it less chewy (although still chewier than other grains) and quicker to cook. Traditionally added to stews and soups.

Ancient wheats such as spelt, emmer, einkorn (collectively called *farro* in Italian) and khorasan are more nutritious than modern wheat and higher in protein. They are known as 'covered wheats' as their kernels do not break free from the outer husk during threshing and so have to be removed mechanically, making them more expensive than modern wheat. They can be prepared in the same way as (and in recipes, substituted for) wheat grain.

know your pulses

Pulses are dry, edible seeds that grow inside a pod, and are part of the legume family. For years, I thought I didn't like pulses because I didn't like kidney beans (they have a particularly strong flavour and noticeable texture). Don't make the same mistake that I did! What a revelation it was to find that chickpeas were mild and fresh, red lentils almost dissolved into the sauces I was making and black-eyed beans were creamy and smooth. Every pulse is different! (I still don't like kidney beans.)

Pulses can be grouped by their characteristics:

+ Lentils are smaller, round and biconvex in shape.
+ Split peas look like lentils, but are peas that have been dried and split in half. They usually have a curved side and a flat side.
+ Peas are round; chickpeas have the characteristics and appearance of a pea although they are known as garbanzo beans in the USA and Canada.
+ Beans are larger than lentils, and are oval or kidney shaped.

Not only do ready-cooked pulses at the store come in a plastic-lined metal tin, they often have added sugar and salt and a slightly slimy texture, and they rarely taste as good as freshly cooked. Dried pulses can seem intimidating, but they are actually simple to prepare. If you can boil water to make pasta, you can cook pulses.

A can of beans is usually 400 g (15 oz), and the drained weight is 240 g (8.5 oz). If a recipe calls for a can of pulses, you'll need around 240 g of your cooked pulses. With pulses that take a long time to cook, I always cook more than I need because they keep a week in the fridge and freeze really well. To freeze, allow to cool after cooking and draining, pop into glass jars (I use jars of a similar size to a can) and keep in the freezer.

A pressure cooker can greatly reduce the amount of time it takes to cook beans (from an hour to just 15 minutes). Note that older beans can also take longer to cook.

Soaking pulses: generally speaking, lentils, split peas and the smallest beans don't require soaking although it is often recommended to reduce the cooking time and aid digestion. Larger beans require soaking, and the larger a bean is the more soaking it requires.

Soaking can be done overnight or first thing in the morning; if your plans change and you no longer have time to cook the pulses, simply change the water and keep them soaking. You can pop them in the fridge at this soaking stage for a couple of days, or leave at room temperature and just change the water every 8 hours or so. I deliberately soak my chickpeas for three days before cooking; I find they are easier to digest and keep their shape more once cooked (which I like). Expect your pulses to swell 2–3 times their initial size while soaking.

If you soak your pulses for long enough (and change the water regularly), eventually they will sprout! Once sprouted, they can be eaten raw, added to salads and cooked in stir fries (you eat the whole thing, including the 'bean' part). They are fresh, crunchy, flavoursome and far superior to the sprouts we buy at the store. Easy pulses to sprout are mung beans, adzuki beans, chickpeas and whole lentils. You don't need to keep them submerged either, just damp. Rinse 1–2 times daily until they sprout.

guide to pulses

Fuss level +
No soaking required,
cooking time 30 minutes or less

Fuss level + +
Soaking may be required,
cooking time 30–60 minutes

Fuss level + + +
Overnight soaking required,
cooking time 60 minutes or more

French green (Puy) and beluga (black) lentils
+
Small lentils that stay very firm when cooked. Great served with roasted beetroot and butternut squash, with a side of sautéed greens. Stir cooked lentils through cooked rice to add extra protein to your meal.

Red lentils
+
Small red-orange lentil, usually sold split. They soften easily, making them good for soup, stews and dal. I use these to make a red lentil ragu: finely chop 2 onions and grate 3 carrots; gently fry on a low heat for 20 minutes. Add 500 g/1 lb 2 oz red lentils, 2 bay leaves and 8 chopped tomatoes, cover with water and cook for 30 minutes until completely soft. Add fresh oregano, parsley or basil and serve with pasta, rice or another grain.

Moong dal
(split mung beans, sometimes called green gram or petite yellow lentils)
+
Small yellow oval pulses that are easily digestible. Dal (or dhal) is a common name for lentils, peas or beans that have been split, although it can also be the name for a spiced dish made using these pulses: cook with finely sliced onion, chopped tomatoes, stock and plenty of spices.

Black beans (turtle beans)

+ +

A small oval shiny black bean with a dense, meaty texture, often used in vegetarian dishes and sometimes in place of pinto beans in Mexican food.

Green and brown lentils

+ +

Medium-sized brown lentils (ranging from khaki to brown) and larger matt green lentils that do not need to be soaked and hold their shape reasonably well when cooked. Both cheaper pulses, making a good replacement for Puy and beluga lentils.

Green/yellow split peas

+ +

A type of pea grown specifically to be dried, then split. The green are slightly sweeter and less starchy than the yellow peas (which look similar to split chickpeas). Soaking is not necessary but will reduce cooking time. Used in soups and to make dal.

Mung beans

+ +

A small green oval-shaped bean with a sweet flavour and soft texture. One of the easiest legumes to digest, and the easiest bean to make sprouts with (turn to page 165 for sprouting instructions).

guide to pulses

Adzuki beans
+ +
Small oval dark red beans, often used in Asian desserts as well as savoury dishes. A great bean to sprout, although slower than mung beans.

Borlotti beans (sometimes called romano beans)
+ + +
A larger, light-brown bean with deep red speckles. Widely used in Italian cooking, with a slightly sweet flavour and smooth, creamy texture.

Black-eyed beans
+ +
A small creamy white bean with a distinctive black spot on one side. Popular in Southern US stews and other dishes. These beans also make a great chickpea substitute.

Chickpeas
(garbanzo beans)
+ + +
Round and angular pulses, usually a pale golden colour. Cooking time is 90 minutes (without a pressure cooker) and the leftover cooking water (called aquafaba) is an excellent egg replacement in baking. Despite chickpeas taking a while to cook, they are one of my favourites because they are so versatile – turn to page 170 for some ideas.

Lima beans

(also called butter beans, white kidney beans, cannellini beans or haricot beans)

+ + +

Large white kidney-shaped beans, lima beans are meatier than navy beans, and retain their texture and shape well. Often used in dishes like minestrone, or in salads or stews.

Pinto beans

+ + +

Kidney-shaped orange-brown beans with red speckles, used in refried beans and burritos.

Navy beans

(also called haricot beans)

+ + +

Small oval white beans, slightly flattened with a shiny skin. Traditionally used to make baked beans, they are creamy when cooked so can be used in dips, for thickening soups and as an alternative to mashed potato.

Kidney beans

+ + +

Large dark-red kidney-shaped beans. They are firm when cooked, with a strong flavour, and are often used in chilli.

6 things you can do with chickpeas (garbanzo beans)

+ Make hummus (page 193) – hummus also freezes really well, so make extra and freeze for later. Hummus is a great way to use up an oversupply of vegetables. Not only can excess cucumbers, carrots, capsicum/peppers and celery be chopped into sticks (crudités) for dipping, but leftover roasted vegetables (such as sweet potato or beetroot) can be blended into the hummus.
+ Sauté onion and diced aubergine/eggplant until soft, add some chopped tomatoes and chickpeas, flavour with cinnamon and ground coriander and serve with rice.
+ Stir-fry some greens with lots of garlic, and toss through two big handfuls of chickpeas; serve with crusty bread or quinoa.
+ Add to fresh salads (cucumber, fresh tomatoes and chickpeas are a great combination with lots of fresh herbs) and squeeze lemon juice over the top.
+ For a savoury snack, sprinkle cooked chickpeas with your favourite spices (I love cumin and turmeric) and salt, drizzle with oil, then place on a baking tray and roast in the oven at 200 °C (400 °F) for 30–40 minutes until crunchy.
+ For a sweet snack, blend 1½ cups cooked chickpeas with ½ cup peanut butter (or other nut butter), ¼ cup liquid sweetener, pinch of salt and 1 tablespoon vanilla extract. Stir through 60 g (2 oz) chocolate chips, nuts or dried fruit. Roll into small balls, place on a baking tray, press down with a fork and bake in the oven at 180 °C (350 °F) for 15 minutes until golden.

If you like firm chickpeas, soak for longer before cooking. If you like mushy chickpeas (or want super-smooth hummus) add a teaspoon of sodium bicarbonate (baking soda) to the soaking water, and another teaspoon to the cooking water.

<u>DIY vanilla extract</u>: slice a vanilla pod (or two) lengthways, pop in a small jar and cover with vodka, brandy or rum (whichever you have). The vanilla will infuse the alcohol, with the flavour developing over time. Allow a few weeks before the first use. When running low, top up with more alcohol (up to two more times). When it's done, dry out the vanilla pods in the oven and blend to a powder for use in baking recipes.

know your vegetables

There are so many fruit and vegetable varieties in the world, and what is available in the store just scratches the surface. I've seen eggplants (aubergines) that are round, elongated, egg-shaped and finger-shaped, coloured white, yellow and orange as well as the familiar dark purple, and even stripy. Kale isn't just the one type: there are dark green, lighter green, black, purple and curly varieties. Sweet potato can be pink, cauliflower can be yellow, potatoes can be blue, tomatoes can be orange, and so it goes on. Not only that, with every colour variation comes a unique taste. So don't write off an entire vegetable just because the one varietal you tried wasn't to your liking!

Vegetables can be classified according to the parts that we eat. This can be helpful when trying to figure out how we might use something new, or what to switch in a recipe. Some vegetables can straddle several categories – for example the leaves of cauliflower and broccoli (the heads are considered flowers) can also be eaten. (Vegetables can also be classified botanically, which is helpful to know when growing our own, but less useful when it comes to cooking.)

Bulbs

Onions, garlic, shallots (which look like onions but multiply like garlic), spring onions/scallions and leeks – these are all members of the same family, and have similar flavours. Fennel is also a bulb, but isn't interchangeable with onions in recipes (it has a mild aniseed flavour).

Fruits

Eggplant/aubergine, tomatoes, tomatillos and capsicum/peppers are edible fruits from the nightshade family; cucumbers, zucchini/courgettes, and pumpkin/squash varieties are from the cucurbit family. Other examples are avocado, plantain and olives.

Flowers

Broccoli, Romanesco broccoli and cauliflower are flowers from the brassica (cabbage) family; globe artichokes are also flowers. Then there are flowers that look like flowers (zucchini blossoms, nasturtiums, pansies, calendula).

Stems

Vegetables that are grown for the stalk include celery, asparagus and kohlrabi. Other vegetables may have edible stems even if this is not what they are grown for – for example broccoli. Bean sprouts fit into this group.

Leaves/leafy greens

Vegetables grown for the leaves include cabbage, kale, Asian greens, spinach, lettuces, mustard greens, rocket/arugula and herbs (such as parsley, coriander/cilantro and mint). Lighter coloured, soft and young leaves can be eaten raw; older and darker leaves are better cooked.

Root vegetables

Carrots, parsnips, beetroot, celeriac, radishes, swedes and turnips all come from plants whose main root swells to produce an edible vegetable.

Tubers

Potatoes, sweet potato/kumara, Jerusalem (sun) artichokes, yams and cassava are tubers – swollen, starchy root growths.

Seeds (peas and beans)

The edible seeds (and sometimes pods) of plants, usually higher in protein than other vegetable types. Sweetcorn, peas and broad beans are seeds; green beans, runner beans, sugar snap peas and okra are examples where the pod is also eaten.

how to cook vegetables

There is so much more to vegetables than boiling them. If you've tried a vegetable cooked one way and didn't like it, don't be afraid to try a different way. Experiment!

Braise/poach

Vegetables are cooked in a small amount of liquid in a pan covered with a lid. Rather than water, the liquid is often stock, broth, wine or milk. Think of it as halfway between boiling and steaming and with extra flavour. Typically poaching is for a short time; braising is for longer. Both delicious.

Try this: leeks (washed, halved lengthways) covered in fragrant stock or white wine with a bay leaf, and poached for 20 minutes on a low heat; or red cabbage braised in red wine and orange juice – infinitely tastier than the boiled version!

Bake

Cooking in the oven, but at a lower temperature than roasting, and food is often covered, which prevents browning and crispy edges. Also a common name for vegetables cooked in the oven in a sauce.

Try this: layer thinly sliced potato, tomato and eggplant/aubergine in a baking dish with plenty of Italian herbs, drizzle with oil and top with breadcrumbs then bake in the oven on medium heat.

Roast

Cooking in oil in a medium–hot oven, usually uncovered. The edges of the vegetables tend to crisp and brown, and natural sugars will caramelise. We think of roasting as predominantly for potatoes, but many vegetables can be roasted, from carrots to cauliflower to tomatoes. A great way to transform wrinkly veggies.

Try this: place cauliflower florets in a roasting tin, drizzle with olive oil and roast in the oven on medium heat for an hour until the edges are crispy and the centres are soft.

Sauté/stir-fry/pan-fry

Sautéing and stir-frying are pretty much the same, except stir-frying traditionally uses a wok and higher heat. The chopped vegetables are cooked in a pan over a high heat with a small amount of oil and moved constantly to prevent burning. Pan-frying is usually reserved for whole pieces of food and needs a slightly lower heat and more care so as not to break it up.

Try this: sautéing onions, carrots, capsicum/peppers and broccoli for a quick evening meal. Add some protein (peanuts, tofu, cooked black-eyed beans or whatever you fancy – you'll find a quick satay sauce recipe on page 191) and your favourite spices. Serve with rice, quinoa or another grain.

Steam

The vegetables are placed over boiling water and cooked by steam. You can use a special steamer basket or a regular metal sieve that fits over a pan of boiling water (cover with the pan lid). 'Wilted greens' are usually steamed until they begin to lose their shape. Steaming retains more nutrients than boiling.

Try this: steam dark leafy greens for 5 minutes, squeeze over some lemon juice and sprinkle toasted sesame seeds on top.

Boil/simmer

Cooking vegetables in boiling water. Dense vegetables (potatoes, beetroot) are good boiled. Less robust vegetables break up with vigorous boiling, so simmer at a lower temperature (delicate vegetables such as leafy greens are better steamed). Cook until tender and run under cold water to stop cooking: overboiling causes vegetables (particularly greens) to lose their colour and go grey.

Try this: boil whole beetroot for 30 minutes, then chop into chunks, drizzle with oil, add a few sprigs of rosemary and roast in the oven on medium heat for 20 minutes. You'll get the taste of roasted beetroot without having to wait three hours.

Grill

Cooking vegetables over high heat on a ridged pan (sometimes referred to as a griddle pan) that leaves black stripes on the food and imparts a smoky flavour.

Try this: zucchini/courgette, capsicum/peppers and eggplant/aubergine are all amazing grilled. Smoky eggplant is great in dips (baba ghanoush), salads and even risotto.

basic recipes

When I first decided to reduce my waste, there were some foods I couldn't find without packaging, and some things that were expensive to buy without packaging. I began experimenting with making my own versions. Some things I decided weren't worth my effort – but going through the process made me very appreciative of being able to buy them, and helped me understand the higher price. Other things were so simple and straightforward I couldn't believe I hadn't been making them all along.

The recipes I've shared here are the latter: simple, straightforward basics that I make all the time. Most I've been making since the very start of my less waste journey several years ago. I've also tried to choose ingredients that you're probably familiar with, but used in ways that you might not have thought of or tried before. Not only do I want you to make these recipes, I also want to stoke your curiosity when it comes to using different ingredients. Being creative is a great way to avoid packaging and reduce food waste, and eating your creations is the best part of all.

nut (or seed) butter

Nut or seed butter is great slathered on fresh apple slices or banana for a snack. It also (to my surprise) tastes great with carrot sticks! Store-bought nut butter often has extras added: salt, sugar, vegetable oil and sometimes palm oil. It's really easy (and usually cheaper) to DIY.

Ideally, you'll need a food processor or high-power blender (one that's suitable for grinding solids). You can make nut butter in a pestle and mortar: you'll just need a bit more patience, and you'll make a smaller quantity.

Almost every commercially available nut butter is made from roasted nuts – the flavour is infinitely better. Don't even think about blending raw nuts (or raw seeds) unless you have a top-of-the-range high-power blender.

You can buy roasted nuts (try to find the ones without salt), or you can roast your own: just spread out on a large baking tray and place in the oven on a low–medium heat. I roast nuts at 150 °C (300 °F) for around 15–20 minutes, opening the oven every 5 minutes or so to give them a shake and check on their progress. The aim is lightly coloured and golden, not dark brown or black. They should smell and taste nutty and aromatic – not burned. Softer nuts like pecans take less time and burn more easily. Better to keep the oven temperature low and roast a little longer than scorch them.

Once roasted, allow nuts to cool completely before making butter. Two cups of whole nuts will make approximately a cup of nut butter.

What to do

Add nuts to the blender, and blend. First you'll get coarse crumbs (if you like crunchy nut butter you can take some out of the blender now, and stir it back through at the end). Next come fine crumbs, then a mix that looks doughy, and eventually you'll get smooth, shiny nut butter. When it's glossy, you're done. You can add salt and/or sugar to taste.

Pop into a glass jar. Nut butters store better in the fridge, but most can be kept in the pantry for up to three months.

Peanut butter

The classic nut butter, except peanuts are actually not nuts but legumes (related to pulses) that grow underground. Peanut butter is high in protein.

Almond butter

Make with roasted almonds, and leave the skins on (this is where all the calcium is). Almond butter makes a good peanut butter substitute.

Hazelnut butter

Roast hazelnuts then rub with a tea towel to remove the bitter skins before making into butter. Hazelnut butter is the base for chocolate hazelnut spread (the best way to eat it).

Sunflower seed butter

A mild-flavoured seed butter. A good budget option and an alternative for those with nut allergies. Blend with nuts (try 50:50) to make more affordable nut butters.

Pumpkin seed butter

Green in colour and more flavoursome than sunflower seed butter. Another nut-free option.

Sesame seed butter

Better known as tahini, a runny seed butter with a distinctive flavour. I use it to make a quick pasta sauce (recipe on page 193); also great added to smoothies and interesting to use in baking.

Cashew nut butter

One of the few nut butters that can be made with raw nuts as well as roasted. Mild, buttery and smooth (cashew nuts are naturally low in fibre), it is often used in icing for cakes and as a base for non-dairy creamy sauces. Keep in the fridge.

Macadamia nut butter

Another nut butter that tastes good made with raw nuts as well as roasted. Has a mild flavour and light texture: great on fruit toast and other baked goods in place of dairy butter. Always keep in the fridge.

Coconut butter

The most solid of the nut butters as the oil in coconut is solid at room temperature. Best made with desiccated or shredded coconut, it takes much longer to blend than other nut butters (you'll need a top-of-the-range blender). Great in raw cakes and bliss balls as it binds ingredients together well.

plant milk

It's possible to make plant milk with nuts, seeds, legumes (soy) and even some grains (rice and oats). Plant milks can be used instead of dairy milk in coffee and tea, on cereal and in porridge, in soups, and in some baking recipes (cakes, muffins and pancakes). They won't work as a direct substitute in every recipe, especially dairy-based sauces, because while they look similar, the proteins they contain are completely different and they cook in different ways.

When adding plant milk to black coffee, it's recommended to warm the milk first – this stops it separating, which can ruin a perfectly good cup of coffee.

Cashew nuts are the lowest fuss option for nut milk, as they have very little fibre and don't need straining. Blend 1 cup of soaked cashew nuts with 5 cups water (blend a cup at a time for 30 seconds to ensure there's no lumps). That's it. Will keep in the fridge for 7 days.

nut (and seed) milk

Almond milk is probably the nut milk we are most familiar with, but nut milk can be made with most nuts and seeds, depending on what's locally available and within your budget. Unlike nut butters, nut (and seed) milks are best made with raw nuts.

The instructions below are for almond milk, but can be adapted for whichever nut or seed you have to hand.

Soak 1 cup raw almonds in water overnight. Rinse well, and blend with 1 litre (34 fl oz) water for 2–3 minutes until combined. Strain through cheesecloth/muslin or a clean tea towel to separate the liquid from the pulp. Squeeze the pulp well to ensure all the moisture is released. Store the milk in a glass bottle in the fridge. This makes about 800 ml (27 fl oz) of almond milk.

Do not throw the pulp away! Use a clean knife to scrape it off the cheesecloth and into a container. We'll talk about what we can do with the pulp shortly.

Almond milk will keep 3–5 days in the fridge; other nut milks will keep slightly longer.

coconut milk and cream

The coconut milk we buy in cans is made from the flesh and juice of young coconuts. Most of us don't have access to young coconuts to make our own, but we can make something almost as good using dried (mature) coconut and water. I prefer to use shredded coconut, but desiccated coconut will work too. (Only attempt to use coconut flakes if you have a top-of-the-range blender.)

Place 300 g (10½ oz) shredded coconut in a heatproof bowl (if your blender has a glass or metal jug, you can use that instead). Boil 1 litre (34 fl oz) of water, pour over the coconut and leave to stand for 30 minutes. Blend the coconut and hot water until combined.

Strain the mix into a glass jug using cheesecloth/muslin or a clean tea towel. Squeeze the cloth to ensure all the moisture is removed – you will want to allow it to cool slightly before you do this. Once you've strained every drop out of the pulp, pour the coconut milk into a glass jar, and screw on the lid. Allow to cool then place in the fridge.

(Once in the fridge, the solids will separate from the liquid. If you'd like to use the coconut cream, you can scoop off using a spoon. Alternatively, if you prefer coconut milk, when you're ready to use it, empty the entire jar contents into a pan and gently warm to recombine.)

Now place the coconut pulp back into the blender (or heatproof bowl), and add another litre (34 fl oz) of boiling water. Leave to sit for 5 minutes, and repeat the process. The second batch will be thinner, with only a very thin layer of coconut cream – great for adding to smoothies instead of water, for cooking grains (quinoa, white rice or millet will absorb the coconut flavour), or adding to soups or dal.

Coconut cream, milk and pulp will keep 3–5 days in the fridge. Suitable for freezing.

oat milk

A popular choice because oats are very affordable, readily available and often locally grown. Oat milk can go slimy if overblended, so it is best not to pre-soak the oats. Avoid using instant oats as these have been pre-cooked.

Add 1 cup rolled oats (jumbo/old-fashioned/unstabilised are best) to a blender with 1 litre (34 fl oz) of water. Blend for 1 minute only. Strain through cheesecloth/muslin or a clean tea towel, and save the pulp. Store the milk in a glass jar in the fridge for 4–5 days.

to strain or not to strain?

Unless you're using it in coffee, tea or hot drinks, or if you don't mind lumps, there's actually no need to strain most plant milks (coconut milk is a definite exception).

If you do want to strain, leftover plant milk pulp can be added to smoothies, stews, curries, cereal or porridge. Small amounts (up to ½ cup) can be smuggled into most muffin, cookie and cake recipes. Try the cracker or macaroon recipes opposite as starting points.

Leftover pulp contains moisture so will last in the fridge only a few days. If you're not going to use it within that time, you have two options: freeze it, or dry it. To freeze, simply pop in a suitable container in the freezer. To oven dry, spread out over a baking tray and place in the oven on a very low heat (100 °C/210 °F or lower), stirring with a wooden spoon every 20–30 minutes (break up clumps as they begin to dry out). Bake for 2 hours or until totally dry, allow to cool completely, whizz briefly in a food processor or blender to separate and store in a glass jar in the pantry for up to a month.

pulp crackers

Mix 1–2 tablespoons of olive or
other oil into 1 cup of leftover pulp,
add water as needed, plus a good
pinch of salt, and spread out on a
baking tray. Press down with the
back of a spoon, then roll out with
a rolling pin. If the pulp is sticky,
placing a silicone sheet or square
of baking paper on top of the pulp
and rolling over that can help. Bake
in the oven for 15 minutes at 160 °C
(320 °F), then remove and score
the surface to create square
cracker shapes. Return to the
oven and continue baking until
completely dry. Separate into
squares, and store in an airtight
container.

pulp macaroons

Place 1 cup of leftover pulp
in a bowl with a bit of water,
2 teaspoons of honey/rice malt
syrup/maple syrup, 1 mashed
banana, a good pinch of salt,
good pinch of cinnamon and
2 tablespoons of flavourless oil,
coconut oil or nut butter and
mix until combined. Press into
flattened balls about an inch
across, and bake in the oven at
150 °C (300 °F) for 30–40 minutes.

crackers

If there's one thing that is hard to find plastic-free, it's crackers. Here are two ideas for making your own.

If you're serving dips or a platter, you could consider skipping the crackers altogether and serving fresh crusty bread or vegetable sticks (crudités) – carrot, capsicum/peppers, celery, cucumber and zucchini/courgette are all great choices.

no baking-skills-required crackers

These are a great way to use up baguettes, ideally 1–2 days old so that they are slightly dried out. Technically they aren't crackers – the Italian name is crostini (in Australia they are called 'crustini'). They sound fancy – and they are expensive to buy pre-packaged – but are simple to make and taste great.

Preheat the oven to 180 °C (350 °F).

Cut the baguette into thin slices about ½ cm (¼ in) thick using a bread knife. If the bread is fresh, dry it out in the oven for a few minutes on a low temperature before slicing.

Lay the slices out on a baking tray, drizzle with olive oil and sprinkle a little salt and pepper over the top. The oil doesn't need to be spread evenly. Bake in the oven for 15 minutes, remove from the oven, flip over and bake on the other side for a further 10 minutes. Cool on a cooling rack, then store in an airtight container. Will keep for a few weeks.

seed crackers

If we're going to go to the trouble of making our own crackers, best to make them as delicious (and nutritious) as possible. This makes enough mix for one baking tray. Depending on how many trays (and oven shelves) you have, double or triple the recipe – it will be much more efficient.

+ 70 g (2½ oz) sunflower seeds
+ 30 g (1 oz) sesame seeds
+ 25 g linseeds (flax seeds)
+ 20 g (¾ oz) pumpkin seeds
+ 15 g (½ oz) chia seeds
+ good pinch of salt
+ 160 ml (5½ fl oz) water

Preheat your oven to 180 °C (350 °F).

Mix all the ingredients in a bowl, and leave to stand for at least 30 minutes (longer is fine) until gloopy.

Line your baking tray(s) with a silicone baking mat or parchment/baking paper.

Pour the seed mix onto the tray and spread thinly and evenly with the back of a spoon (if using baking paper, work quickly), trying to avoid making holes.

Place the tray in the oven and bake for 30–40 minutes. Remove from the oven and score with a knife to outline the crackers. (Once they are fully baked they will not cut without shattering, so the lines need to be marked while the mixture is still soft.)

Return to the oven for 30 minutes. Check and remove any crackers that are cooked (the middle will take longer than the edges). If possible, separate the uncooked crackers to speed up final cooking and return to the oven.

Cook for another 15–30 minutes or until the crackers are completely dry, crisp and crunchy. To dry out further, the crackers can be left in the warm oven once it is turned off. Remove from the oven and cool completely on a rack. Store in an airtight container.

When crackers go soft, you can restore their crunch by baking them in the oven on low–medium heat for about 15 minutes.

sauces and dips

Sauces and dips are a great way to jazz up leftover vegetables, and make a meal more exciting. These 'cheat' options don't require any skill or long preparation time: simply mix together the ingredients and you're good to go.

Rather than using a jar of tomato sauce or even a can of tomatoes when a recipe calls for them, I simply use 5-6 Roma/plum tomatoes, roughly chopped. They'll take slightly longer to cook (canned tomatoes have been blanched already) but the end result is almost the same.

satay sauce

A simple sauce made from peanut butter that will next-level any stir-fried vegetables. I make it to use straightaway, but it will keep in the fridge for a few days too. You can swap out peanut butter for almond butter, if you prefer.

Serves 2

+ 4 tablespoons peanut butter
+ 1 tablespoon apple cider vinegar (lemon or lime juice will also work)
+ 80 ml (2½ fl oz) coconut cream or 60 ml (2 fl oz) plant milk
+ 2 teaspoons soy sauce or tamari
+ 5 g (¼ oz) fresh ginger or ½ teaspoon ground ginger
+ 1 teaspoon sugar (honey/rice malt syrup/maple syrup)
+ pinch of chilli powder or cayenne pepper

Mix the peanut butter with the vinegar. Slowly add the coconut cream or plant milk and stir until combined. Add the other ingredients and adjust to taste.

If you are using plant milk instead of coconut cream you might want to add more peanut butter to make it thicker.

tahini sauce

A simple sauce made with tahini (sesame seed butter) that is great as a dipping sauce or drizzled on salads (add 1 teaspoon of honey and ½ teaspoon ground cumin to make a salad dressing). For a quick and easy meal, stir-fry onion, garlic, broccoli, mushrooms and kale in a pan in some olive oil, place on top of cooked pasta and drizzle with tahini sauce.

+ juice of ½ lemon
+ 65 g (2¼ oz/ ¼ cup) tahini
+ 60 ml (2 fl oz/ ¼ cup) plant or dairy milk

Mix the lemon juice in with the tahini. It will seize up and become thicker. Then, slowly add the milk until you reach your desired consistency – less makes a thick dipping sauce (great for falafel), more makes a runnier sauce. Add salt and pepper to taste.

Lemons not in season? Switch for the same quantity of apple cider vinegar (DIY recipe on page 203).

hummus

I don't add oil to my hummus because I use a lot of tahini, which is high in oil. Don't have (or like) chickpeas? Try black-eyed beans, navy beans or other beans of your choice instead.

+ 300 g (10½ oz) cooked chickpeas
+ 100 g (3½ oz) tahini (I use hulled tahini; unhulled tahini is slightly darker and slightly bitter)
+ 1–2 garlic cloves, crushed and finely chopped
+ juice of ½ lemon

Blend the chickpeas, tahini, garlic and lemon juice together (a food processor or blender will be faster, but a pestle and mortar will also do the trick). The hummus will be very thick; add small amounts of water, bit by bit, and blend until you reach your preferred consistency.

Flavoured hummus: to the ingredients above, add 1 large/2 small cooked beetroot (or grated raw beetroot), or 1–2 roasted capsicum/peppers, or 2–3 roasted carrots (I add cumin to this), or a big handful of greens. Experiment!

pesto four ways

The word pesto comes from the Italian word *pestare*, which means 'to pound, or crush'. It is a great way to use up leafy greens: basil, rocket/arugula, carrot tops, parsley, coriander/cilantro, kale, spinach, nasturtium leaves or whatever we find in the fridge (or the garden). Limp leaves make fine pesto.

My formula for pesto is greens, garlic, nuts or seeds, oil and sometimes lemon juice or apple cider vinegar. I don't use cheese: if I want a cheesy flavour, I add nutritional yeast flakes purchased from the bulk store.

Pesto whizzes up quickly in a food processor, but a pestle and mortar will also work. These recipes make one jar of pesto, but you can easily double them (I often do): it's the same amount of washing up, and pesto freezes well so you can save half for a quick meal another day. Any pesto you are not eating or freezing straightaway will keep in a glass jar in the fridge for 5 days.

parsley & walnut pesto

I often make this in the colder months when basil isn't available for traditional summer pesto. Basil leaves bruise easily and darken, but this parsley pesto stays a brilliant bright green.

Makes 1 jar

+ 3 garlic cloves
+ 3 large handfuls flat-leaf/Italian parsley
+ 100 g (3½ oz/ 1 cup) walnuts
+ 250 ml (8½ fl oz/ 1 cup) olive oil
+ 3 tablespoons nutritional yeast

Chop the garlic, then blend with the parsley to make a paste. Add the walnuts and blend again, then mix in the oil until combined. Finally, stir in the nutritional yeast.

nasturtium & almond pesto

Nasturtium leaves are peppery, and can be switched out for rocket (arugula) or another fiery leaf. If it's too strong, consider swapping half of the nasturtium for a mild green leaf like spinach.

Makes 1 jar

+ 1–2 garlic cloves
+ 3 large handfuls nasturtium leaves
+ 80 g (2¾ oz/ ½ cup) almonds
+ 250 ml (8½ fl oz/ 1 cup) olive oil
+ juice of 1 lemon

Chop the garlic, then blend with the nasturtium leaves to make a paste. Add the almonds, blend again, then mix in the oil and lemon juice until combined.

carrot tops pesto

I often use avocado in pesto recipes to replace some of the oil as a healthier alternative. If you don't have avocado, you can use more olive oil.

Makes 1 jar

+ 9 Brazil nuts
+ 50 g (1¾ oz/⅓ cup) cashew nuts
+ 1 large garlic clove
+ 1 large handful basil
+ 2 large handfuls carrot tops
+ 2 tablespoons olive oil
+ ½ avocado
+ ⅓ cup nutritional yeast (optional)

Chop the Brazil nuts (or blend in a food processor) until they resemble coarse breadcrumbs, and set aside. Do the same with the cashew nuts.

Chop the garlic, then blend with the basil leaves and carrot tops to make a fine paste. Add the oil and avocado and blend again. Add the cashew nuts and blend. Add the Brazil nuts and nutritional yeast, if using, and stir to combine. Add more oil if required to achieve desired consistency.

coriander & cashew pesto

Coriander and cashew pesto has a distinct Thai flavour to it. While most pesto recipes will benefit from adding cheese or nutritional yeast to them, this one will definitely not!

Makes 1 jar

+ 1–2 garlic cloves
+ 4 large handfuls coriander/ cilantro
+ 235 g (8½ oz/ 1½ cups) cashew nuts
+ 185 ml (6 fl oz/ ¾ cup) macadamia oil (or other flavourless oil)

Chop the garlic, then blend with the coriander to make a paste. Add the cashew nuts and blend again. Finally, add the oil and mix until combined.

__The type of nut__ or seed used can wildly affect the cost of the final pesto. Try your own versions using what's local to you and within your budget.

pesto is not only for pasta!

+ Stir some pesto through cooked, cooled rice (or other grain) to make a pesto salad.
+ Use as a dip for crackers or crudités.
+ Remove the stalks from closed-cup mushrooms, chop the stalks finely and stir through pesto. Place the mushrooms upside down on a baking tray, fill the cups with a tablespoon of pesto mixture and top with breadcrumbs. Bake in the oven on medium heat for 20 minutes until cooked.
+ Spread a thin layer of pesto on toast and top with cooked mushrooms, tomatoes and/or more greens sautéed with garlic.
+ Cut some potatoes into cubes, cook (roasted or boiled are both great) and stir through pesto to make a warm potato salad – or leave to cool, and serve chilled.

what do I do with:
'sad' food?

Black bananas

Use to make banana bread or add to smoothies. They also freeze well, either in their skins or peeled and placed in a suitable container. Blending frozen bananas with peanut butter makes a delicious soft-serve ice cream.

Dry bread

Freeze bread that's no longer fresh, and use for toast (you can toast bread straight from the freezer). Dry or stale bread can be used to make breadcrumbs: dry out in the oven, whizz in a blender or crush in a pestle and mortar, then store in the pantry or freeze. Dry baguettes can be used to make easy crackers that will keep for a few months in an airtight container – just follow the directions on page 189.

Limp greens

Chop until fine and add to stews, dal or sauces. They will reduce and you won't notice them. Alternatively, make a batch of pesto. Strong leafy greens like rocket/arugula can be used on their own; mix mild greens like lettuce with a strong-flavoured herb like basil to give your pesto flavour.

Mouldy cheese

It's actually safe to cut mould off hard cheese. If you notice white spots on your cheese it may not be mould at all but calcium lactate, a salt that is completely harmless (it's common on cheddar and colby).

Separated yoghurt

It's common for the curds (solid) and whey (liquid) to separate in yoghurt, but this doesn't mean it's bad. Draining the whey is how Greek yoghurt and labne cheese are made. Either stir the yoghurt to recombine, or drain off the whey (the yoghurt will be thicker).

Sour milk	This can be used in baking as a substitute for buttermilk; the acidity actually improves the flavour of some baked goods. (The souring is not caused by food poisoning bacteria, so it is safe to consume.)
Wrinkly/old fruit	Chop and simmer on the stove in a small amount of water to make stewed fruit (add sugar and spices as needed: cinnamon and ginger are both delicious) and stir through porridge or yoghurt. Stewed fruit can also be frozen. Alternatively, slice the fruit, cover with crumble topping and bake in the oven.
Wrinkly vegetables	Wilting is caused by water loss, so make the most of this and roast your bendy veggies. Drizzle carrots, capsicum/peppers, zucchini/courgettes and tomatoes with oil and pop in the oven on a high temperature to bring out the flavour. Roasted vegetables freeze really well.

what do I do with:
leftovers?

Pasta   Cover with a fresh batch of sauce and bake, add to tomato-based soups, or stir some pesto through for an easy snack.

Rice   Cold rice works really well in stir-fries: add to the wok when the vegetables are cooked and stir through. Or combine with cooked lentils and heaps of fresh herbs to make a simple rice salad. Rice freezes well.

Protein   Stir-fry with a selection of fresh vegetables; or add to sauces, soups or salads to fill them out.

Vegetables   Add to salads, sauces, stir-fries or stews, or eat as a snack.

Sauces   Add to a stew or soup, or bulk out with some new vegetables and protein to make sauce version 2.0.

what do I do with: 'scraps'?

Beetroot leaves

Can be used in the same way as other leafy greens: add to sauces or stews, or stir-fry. Young beetroot leaves can be used in salads. They have a slightly salty taste.

Broccoli stems and leaves

Both edible and delicious. If the stalk is tough, cut the outer skin off and use the softer middle. Chop and use as you would use broccoli.

Citrus rind

The coloured part of the rind is bursting with flavour. Peel the fruit with a sharp knife or peeler, and either dry or freeze in strips, or finely chop and freeze. Can be used in baking, and to flavour rice, stews and salads.

Pumpkin seeds

These tasty morsels are too good for the bin. When preparing pumpkin, put the seeds and stringy insides in a bowl of water and agitate to loosen the seeds. Spread over a baking tray and dry in the oven (pop in a hot but turned-off oven once you've finished cooking). The white husk can be eaten, or split open with your teeth to find the green pumpkin seed inside.

Vegetable peels

Rather than peeling your root vegetables, scrub well instead. If you prefer to peel your vegetables (or need to for a particular recipe), toss the peels in some olive oil, lay out on a baking tray and cook in the oven for 10–15 minutes on medium temperature until crispy. Fresh vegetable chips! Carrot and potato peels work particularly well.

what do I do with: vegetable trimmings?

Save in a glass jar or reusable silicone bag in the freezer to make stock. Pop the scraps in a pan, add some herbs (1–2 bay leaves plus a small amount of fresh herbs), cover with water, bring to the boil and simmer for an hour. Strain (compost the scraps) and pour into glass jars. Cool, then keep in the fridge or freezer, and use to cook grains, braise vegetables and make soups, dal or risotto.

Great vegetables for making stock:

+ Onions
+ Leeks
+ Carrots

+ Celery
+ Parsnips
+ Mushrooms

+ Corncobs
  (kernels removed)
+ Tomatoes

Not-so-great vegetables for making stock:

+ Cabbage, broccoli, kale stalks (anything from the brassica family can make stock bitter)

+ Beetroot and beetrot peels (very overwhelming and make the stock very dark)

Because corncobs are bulky, I tend to make corn stock immediately after cooking fresh corn. Boil the corn in a pan of hot water for 2 minutes until the corn is a rich golden yellow. Take the cobs out of the water with tongs, then cut away all the cooked corn kernels with a sharp knife, ready to eat. Scrape any bits of loose corn still on the cobs into the pan you just used to cook the corn, and then add the bare cobs and perhaps a couple of bay leaves. Boil the corncobs for 30 minutes. If not using straightaway, allow to cool, then chill. Can also be frozen.

what do I do with: apple cores?

Can be used to make apple cider vinegar (pear cores will make pear cider vinegar). If you intend to save the cores for vinegar, you might prefer to cut the flesh from the core with a knife rather than using your teeth. Pop the cores and/or peels of 6–8 apples in a 1 litre (2 pint) jar of water, add 1–2 tablespoons of sugar, cover with a clean cloth and leave on the counter for 2–3 weeks, stirring occasionally. Bubbles will appear, the sugar will turn to alcohol (cider), the alcohol to vinegar and then you're done (the solids will sink when it's ready).

Sub apple cider vinegar into any recipes that require lemon juice for acidity. You can also use apple cider vinegar to make refrigerator pickles (just know that it will darken most fruits and vegetables more than white vinegar). I also use apple cider vinegar to make this easy wholegrain mustard.

easy mustard

+ ½ cup whole yellow mustard seeds (or a mix of yellow and black)
+ 125 ml (4 fl oz/ ½ cup) apple cider vinegar
+ 1 teaspoon salt
+ 2 teaspoons liquid sweetener: honey/maple syrup/rice malt syrup/ coconut nectar

Grind half of the seeds to a powder in a pestle and mortar (or spice grinder). Mix the mustard powder, remaining seeds and vinegar together in a jar. Leave on the counter for 24 hours, stirring occasionally. Add salt and sweetener, and adjust to taste. Keeps 3–4 months in the fridge.

food preservation

Before fridges and freezers were invented, people had to come up with other ways to stop food going bad. And they did. There are so many different ways to preserve food, and the best are often also the simplest. Most don't need fancy equipment – you can make ferments with just a jar, jams and chutneys with a saucepan and dehydrate food in an oven.

Don't make the mistake of thinking that preserving is only for gardening enthusiasts, homesteaders or anyone with too much time on their hands. It can be a quick and fuss-free way to use a glut of something, and is particularly useful when fridge and/or freezer space is limited, as preserved food can usually be stored at room temperature. Preserving can be a fun way to spend an hour (or less) in the kitchen on a rainy weekend. Plus you'll be hard pressed to find a chutney or preserve in the store that tastes better than one you make yourself, and homemade preserves make great (and interesting) gifts.

The purpose of food preservation techniques is to extend the life of food by preventing 'bad' microorganisms (bacteria, yeasts and mould) from growing, and slowing down oxidation. To go into preserving methods in detail would require a whole other book (and believe me, there are plenty on the subject). Instead I'll introduce some different methods, how they work and what they're used for. See this as a springboard to discovery!

It can be tempting to want to cut down the sugar or salt in preserving recipes because it always seems like a lot. Sugar and salt are preserving ingredients and reducing the quantity may reduce the shelf life of the product you make. Feel free to adjust spices, but avoid adjusting sugar, salt or acid ingredients.

preserving
(fuss level +)

The most well-known preserves are jams, which are spreads made by boiling fruit and sugar together until thick. Sugar is a natural preservative that removes the moisture available for microorganisms to grow. Chutneys are also preserves, but use vinegar and less sugar, and might consist of vegetables as well as or instead of fruit.

Jam and chutney recipes sometimes suggest you use a maslin (or preserving) pan. This is a big stainless steel pan with an extra-thick bottom that helps prevent sugar from burning on the base. You don't need one, especially if you're making small batches; use a regular saucepan and make sure you stir often to stop sugar catching on the bottom and burning.

How to sterilise your equipment: wash jars, lids, and any other tools in hot soapy water, rinse off any soap and drain (don't dry with a tea towel). Preheat the oven to 120 °C (250 °F). Place the jars upright on an oven tray (I find this makes it easier to get them in and out of the oven) or directly on the oven shelves, and leave in the oven for 15 minutes. It's fine to put slightly wet jars in the oven, just ensure they are completely dry before removing them (this may take a few extra minutes). Bring a pan of water to the boil on the stovetop, then add the lids and any tools that you'll be handling the preserves with. Allow to boil for 5 minutes, then turn off the heat and leave in the water until ready to use.

Alternatively, equipment and jars can be sterilised by putting through a hot wash in your dishwasher (without dishwashing detergent), if you have one.

jams, jellies and marmalade

Jams can be made from as little as two ingredients (a single fruit type and sugar) and take about 20 minutes to cook. Pectin helps jams to set (thicken), but if you're not worried about a slightly runnier consistency it's easy to make with just regular granulated sugar. Acid such as lemon juice can also help with setting. Jams can be stored for up to a year.

You can use pretty much any type of fruit, and add your favourite spices (such as ginger, cardamom or cinnamon) for extra flavour. Making jam with berries is a great way to use up a glut, and marmalade makes use of the citrus peels as well as the flesh.

Jellies are similar to jam but made with the juice of the fruit so the resulting preserve is free from skins and seeds. The fruit is usually briefly cooked in water, mashed and then strained – the liquid is then cooked with sugar in the same way as jam.

chutneys

Chutney is a preserve made with sugar and vinegar, less sweet than jam and often used to accompany savoury food. Chutneys can use fruit (mango chutney is delicious, but most fruits make great chutney) or vegetables (piccalilli is my favourite, a spicy British chutney made with cauliflower and turmeric). In the UK many chutneys are referred to as pickles.

Chutneys can seem intimidating because they often have a longer list of ingredients, but they are made in a similar way to jam. All those extra ingredients add much more depth of flavour: if you find jam too sweet, chutneys are a great alternative to use up excess fruit. The flavour of chutney often matures over time, and some recipes even advise storing for a few months before eating.

dehydrating
(fuss level +)

This involves slicing food and then laying out on trays to dry so no moisture remains. This prevents the growth of microorganisms; it also intensifies the flavour. Sun-drying is one of the oldest forms of food preservation. Dried food can be stored at room temperature, and will last indefinitely.

Food dehydrators have a heat element (to warm the food), a fan (to encourage air circulation), drying racks (which aid air flow) and a thermostat (to keep the temperature constant). If you're just drying the odd thing and can't justify a new appliance, it's possible to use your oven: turn onto the lowest temperature, ensure you're using the fan setting (if you have one) and keep the door slightly ajar to allow moisture to escape. It's also possible to dry food in front of a sunny window, or outside (covered with a fine mesh to stop bugs getting in).

Successful dehydrating requires a consistent low temperature. If food is dried at too high a temperature, the outside becomes hard and dry but the inside remains moist, which can lead to food spoiling.

Fruit is perfect for dehydrating, in slices, halved or even puréed. Fruit leather is fruit (pre-cooked or raw) that has been blended and then spread on a sheet and dried to make a chewy snack. Six pieces of fruit (apples, pears, bananas, stone fruit or whatever you have) can be puréed and dried over a few hours to make a 30 cm × 30 cm (12 in × 12 in) square of fruit leather, which can be cut into six strips, and stored in the pantry for months.

pickling
(fuss level + or +++)

Pickling preserves food in an acidic (low pH) solution, usually vinegar. (Fermentation is a type of pickling, and we'll talk about that separately.) Vinegar is a mild acid (acetic acid) that creates an environment that most microorganisms cannot tolerate.

It's possible to buy 'pickling vinegar'; this is simply white or malt vinegar with salt and spices already added. You can also buy 'pickling spice', which is a mix of various fragrant spices. It's just as easy to use regular vinegar and make your own spice mix.

Many pickling recipes require the vinegar to be heated, often bringing it to the boil. They may require the vegetables to be soaked in brine (which will remove some of the water content). These steps all ensure the pickles last longer.

Some recipes require the pickled vegetables to be canned to ensure they can be safely stored at room temperature. The easiest option is to make refrigerator pickles – pickles that are kept in the fridge.

If you're a beginner, pickled chillies, cucumbers (look up 'bread and butter' pickles), onions and garlic are a great place to start. It's not necessary to sterilise your equipment when making refrigerator pickles but it's good practice, and you're reducing the chance of your food going bad.

<u>Once in the fridge</u>, **pickled garlic may turn blue. This may look alarming but actually it's completely safe to eat. It sometimes happens to garlic in high-acid environments and does not affect the taste.**

fermenting
(fuss level +)

This technique uses good bacteria, yeasts and other microorganisms to transform food and increase its pantry life. Sourdough bread, yoghurt, beer, cider, tempeh, kombucha, chocolate and vinegar are fermented foods you're probably already familiar with, but this barely scratches the surface when it comes to fermentation.

Different ferments are made in different ways. Some are strictly anaerobic (made with no oxygen present – for example, beer or cider), others are still anaerobic but more forgiving (such as pickled vegetables) and a few are aerobic (meaning oxygen is present – for example, a sourdough ferment uses oxygen to make carbon dioxide, and the resulting bubbles cause the bread to rise).

Fermented pickles are those that use salt and naturally occurring lactic acid bacteria ('good' bacteria), instead of vinegar. This type of fermentation is called lacto-fermentation. We don't add acid, we create it (or rather, the lactic acid bacteria do).

We've already talked about how to make a simple ferment on page 203: apple cider vinegar!

If you're a beginner, the easiest foods to start with are vegetables: cabbage, carrots and cucumbers. Fermented cabbage (sauerkraut) is really simple to make with just a glass jar, some cabbage and some salt. Just as simple but a little more interesting is curtido, a South American ferment made from cabbage, onion and carrot with a little chilli.

canning
(fuss level +++)

This involves sealing food in airtight jars, and boiling the jars to sterilise them. Despite the name it's almost always in glass jars or bottles (sometimes it's called bottling). It's necessary for preserves that are lower in sugar or salt, or acid, or if you want to extend the life of your preserves from months to years.

Canning helps prevent against a particularly nasty bacteria, *Clostridium botulinum*, which produces a powerful neurotoxin that causes the rare but dangerous condition botulism. It can go undetected in improperly prepared canned food: you can't see it, smell it or taste it. It will not grow in very high acid foods, but there is a risk with low-acid foods. To kill the spores, food needs to be heated to 121 °C (249 °F) for three minutes.

There are two methods for canning, the water bath method and pressure canning. The first is safe for higher acid foods like fruit, pickles, relishes and sauces made with vinegar; the second is required for low acid foods like vegetables, broth, meat and fish.

Water canning:

Sealed, airtight jars of food are placed on a rack inside a big pan which is filled with water, completely submerging the jars, and brought to the boil (100 °C/212 °F). The jars are processed in boiling water for around 10 minutes or so (the recipe you're following will give the exact details).

Pressure canning:

A pressure canner is a specialist piece of equipment (not the same as a pressure cooker) that uses pressure to increase the water temperature to 121 °C (249 °F) and kill off any unwanted microbes or spores.

a final word

This might seem like the end, but it's also the beginning. Hopefully you have lots of ideas and are feeling confident about your next steps: learning more, experimenting with new things and giving it all a try. There will be wins and there will be fails. There will be good days and bad days. There will be plastic purchased and leftovers forgotten about. Remember, there is no 'perfect', just plenty of ways that we can try to do our bit to reduce our impact, make a difference and enjoy ourselves in the process.

Don't forget that our current food system isn't set up (yet) to make these better ways of doing things accessible to everyone. If you come up against obstacles, or find yourself struggling with something, know that it is not your fault. Embrace those opportunities that you do have. None of us can change this system alone ... but we're not alone.

Together, all doing what we can, we are championing better businesses, encouraging planet-friendly practices and supporting sustainable systems. We're participating in a new, better way of doing things. Our purchases are just one part of that. Our voices are another. Don't be afraid to ask questions, and share what you learn.

We have power in the choices we make and actions we take – and best of all, we can start today.

acknowledgements

I live on Noongar boodja (in the place also known as Perth, Western Australia). The Noongar people from the South West region of Western Australia have lived on and cared for these lands for over 45,000 years. There may be no such thing as 'planetarily perfect' but the way that First Nations peoples, in Australia and everywhere, have and continue to live in balance with their surroundings is as close as it gets. I'd like to pay my respects to all Aboriginal, Torres Strait Islander and other First Nations elders past, present and emerging, thank them for being such diligent and effective custodians of the land, and acknowledge that we all have a lot to learn from them.

For all their hard work, encouragement, patience and cheery enthusiasm I'd like to thank Arwen, Emily, Sonja, Vanessa and Madeline, and all the other people at Hardie Grant who helped take this book from idea to reality.

Finally, thanks to everyone who has been a part of this journey: asking questions, sharing ideas, challenging assumptions, offering solutions and, most of all, taking action. It really takes a community to bring about change.

about the author

Lindsay Miles is a passionate zero-waste and plastic-free-living spokesperson, writer and educator who helps people to find more meaningful lives with less waste and less stuff. She has been sharing ideas and strategies on her popular website, Treading My Own Path, since 2013, and has been featured by the ABC and BBC, Channel 9, *The Guardian*, Seven West Media, *The Sunday Times*, TreeHugger, TEDx and more. She gives talks and workshops to encourage others to embrace change, reconnect with their values and make a positive impact on the world around them.

The Less Waste No Fuss Kitchen is her second book.

endnotes

P. 8. 84 per cent of US shoppers buy their food primarily at a supermarket or supercentre.
Shahbandeh, M, 'Food purchases: US consumers' primary shopping location 2017', Statista, 9 July 2019.

P. 8. In the UK less than 2 per cent of shoppers buy groceries from independent stores.
Wunsch, NG, 'Grocery market share in Great Britain 2015–2019', Statista, 16 October 2019.

P. 8. Coles and Woolworths, along with Aldi make up 73 per cent of the Australian grocery market.
'Customer satisfaction press release', Roy Morgan Research, 23 March 2018.

P. 9. The average supermarket today stocks 40,000–50,000 different product lines.
Malito, A, 'Grocery stores carry 40,000 more items than they did in the 1990s', Marketwatch, 17 June 2017.

P. 9. In 2014 Australians spent almost $20 million on asparagus imported from countries including Peru and Mexico.
'Fresh vegetable imports by vegetable', AUSVEG, May 2017.

P. 9. The USA imported 228,000 tonnes (502.4 million pounds) of asparagus from Mexico, Peru and Chile in 2017.
'Asparagus', Agricultural Marketing Resource Center, June 2018.

P. 9. Transportation of food accounts for around 11 per cent of the greenhouse gases that an average household in the USA or the UK generates annually as a result of food consumption.
Engelhaupt, E, 'Do food miles matter?', ACS Publications, 15 May 2008.

P. 13. There are over 750 varieties of eating apple grown throughout the world.
Elzenbroek, ATG, *Guide to Cultivated Plants*, CABI, 2008.

P. 13. There are at least 300 types of edible banana. Promusa, 2018.

P. 14. Around 5.6 billion pounds (2.5 million tonnes) of pesticides are used worldwide every year, with over 1 billion pounds used in the United States alone.
Alavanja, MCR, 'Pesticide use and exposure extensive worldwide', *Reviews on Environmental Health*, 24(4), October–December 2009, pp. 303–309.

P. 14. It has been estimated that 25 million agricultural workers worldwide experience unintentional pesticide poisonings each year.
Jeyaratnam, J, 'Acute poisoning: a major global health problem', *World Health Statistics Quarterly*, 43(3), 1990, pp. 139–44.

P. 14. The pesticide Paraquat has been linked to Parkinson's disease.
Reczek, CR, Birsoy, K, et al, 'A CRISPR screen identifies a pathway required for paraquat-induced cell death', *Nature Chemical Biology*, 13(12),December 2017, pp. 1274–9.

P. 14. Organophosphates have been linked to lymphoma, leukaemia and childhood cancers.
Hu, L, Luo, D, et al, 'The association between non-Hodgkin lymphoma and organophosphate pesticides exposure: a meta-analysis', *Environmental Pollution*, 231, December 2017, pp. 319–328; Hertz-Picciotto, I, Sass, JB, et al, 'Organophosphate exposures during pregnancy and child neurodevelopment: recommendations for essential policy reforms', *PLOS Medicine*, 15(10), 24 October 2018.

P. 15. An estimated 20–40 per cent of fruit and vegetables are rejected before they reach the supermarket simply because they do not meet cosmetic standards.
Koziol, M, '"Ugly" fruits and vegetables the supermarkets reject', *The Sydney Morning Herald*, 1 April 2015.

P. 16. In 2013 the United Nations declared that if food waste was a country, it would be the third biggest emitting country in the world, behind China and the USA.
'Food wastage footprint & climate change', Food and Agriculture Organization of the United Nations, April 2014.

P. 16. Around 40 per cent of everything the average householder throws away is food waste.
'Food waste fast facts', FoodWise, 2019.

P. 16. Globally it's estimated that one third of all food produced for human consumption never gets eaten.
'Food loss and food waste', Food and Agriculture Organization of the United Nations, 2019.

P. 17. Over 99 per cent of plastic is made from petrochemicals.
'Fuelling plastics: fossils, plastics, & petrochemical foodstocks', Center for International Environmental Law, 21 September 2017.

P. 17. Plastic production is responsible for around 6 per cent of global oil consumption, the same proportion as the global aviation sector.
'The new plastics economy: rethinking the future of plastics', Ellen MacArthur Foundation, 19 January 2016.

P. 17. In 2018 *The Guardian* estimated that British supermarkets alone create more than 800,000 tonnes (1.8 billion pounds) of plastic packaging waste each year.
Laville, S, and Taylor, M, 'Nearly 1m tonnes every year: supermarkets shamed for plastic packaging', *The Guardian*, 18 January 2018.

P. 17. In 2018 *National Geographic* revealed that only 9 per cent of all the plastic ever made has likely been recycled.
Geyer, R, Jambeck, JR, and Law, KL, 'Production, use and fate of all plastics ever made', *Science Advances*, 3(7), 19 July 2017.

PP. 17–18. 406 million tonnes (896 billion pounds) of plastic is produced worldwide every year, of which nearly 40 per cent (146 million tonnes) is used for packaging.
Parker, L, 'Fast facts about plastic pollution', *National Geographic*, 20 December 2018.

P. 42. Without action, there will be more plastic than fish in the ocean by 2050.

'The new plastics economy: rethinking the future of plastics and catalysing action', Ellen MacArthur Foundation, 13 December 2017.

P. 43. More than 40 years after the launch of the first universal recycling symbol, only 14 per cent of plastic packaging is collected for recycling, and after processing only 5 per cent is recycled.
'The new plastics economy: rethinking the future of plastics and catalysing action', Ellen MacArthur Foundation, 13 December 2017.

P. 46. Because oxo-biodegradable plastic offers no environment benefit, its use in single-use plastic products was prohibited in the EU in 2019.
'Directive (EU) 2019/904 of the European Parliament and of the Council of 5 June 2019 on the reduction of the impact of certain plastic products on the environment', *Official Journal of the European Union*, 12 June 2019.

P. 51. Paper bags have three times the carbon footprint of plastic ones.
'Paper vs. plastic bags: the studies', All About Bags, 2012.

P. 61. Packaging accounts for approximately 34 per cent of plastic use in the United States and 40 per cent of plastic use in Europe.
'Fuelling plastics: fossils, plastics, & petrochemical foodstocks', Center for International Environmental Law, 21 September 2017.

P. 78. Our food system is responsible for one quarter of greenhouse gas emissions globally.
Poore, J, and Nemecek, T, 'Reducing food's environmental impacts through producers and consumers', *Science*, 360(6392), 01 June 2018, pp. 987–92.

P. 78. Meat, aquaculture (farming fish and crustaceans), eggs and dairy use around 83 per cent of the world's farmland, contribute 56–58 per cent of food's carbon emissions, provide 37 per cent of our protein and 18 per cent of our calories.
Poore, J, and Nemecek, T, 'Reducing food's environmental impacts through producers and

consumers', *Science*, 360(6392), 1 June 2018, pp. 987–92.

P. 79. A 2015 study concluded that a diet that limits meat consumption to two days a week would reduce carbon emissions by almost half compared with eating meat every day.
Ruini, LF, Ciati, R, et al. 'Working toward healthy and sustainable diets: the "Double Pyramid Model" developed by the Barilla Center for Food and Nutrition to raise awareness about the environmental and nutritional impact of foods', *Frontiers in Nutrition*, 2(9), 4 May 2015.

P. 82. A 2017 study by the journal *Nature* found that to keep climate change at under 2 °C, the average world citizen needed to eat 75 per cent less beef, 90 per cent less pork and half the number of eggs, and citizens of rich nations including the UK and USA needed to cut dairy milk consumption by 60 per cent.
Springmann, M, Clark, M, et al. 'Options for keeping the food system within environmental limits', *Nature*, 562(7728), October 2018, pp. 519–25.

PP. 85-87. Plant foods higher in protein; Calcium from plants; Iron from plants
Food Standards Australia New Zealand Food Composition Database, 2019; US Department of Agriculture Agricultural Research Service, 2019.

PP. 90-91. The Haber-Bosch process, an industrial process that creates nitrogen fertiliser, produces around 450 million tonnes (992 billion pounds) of carbon dioxide emissions every year. That's more than any other chemical-making reaction.
Krietsch Boerner, L, 'Industrial ammonia production emits more CO_2 than any other chemical-making reaction. Chemists want to change that', *Chemical & Engineering News*, 97, 24 June 2019.

P. 91. Before 1920, a US family spent more than 40 per cent of their income on food.
Johnson, DS, Rogers, JM, and Tan, L, 'A century of family budgets in the United States', *Monthly Labor Review*, May 2001.

P. 91. Organic farming not only reduces fossil fuel consumption by avoiding chemical fertilisers, but has been shown to increase soil carbon through the use of natural fertilisers.
Ghabbour et al. 'National Comparison of the Total and Sequestered Organic Matter Contents of Conventional and Organic Farm Soils', *Advances in Agronomy*, 146, 2017, pp. 1-35.

P. 91. By 1960 the average American spent 17 per cent of their income on food, and this has continued to decline to less than 10 per cent today, of which half is eating out.
'Food prices and spending', United States Department of Agriculture Economic Research Service, 20 September 2019.

P. 93. Every year, the US-based Environmental Working Group (EWG) put out a report called the Shoppers Guide to Pesticides in Produce.
'EWG's 2019 Shopper's Guide to Pesticides in Produce™', Environmental Working Group, 20 March 2019.

P. 93. The most frequently detected pesticide, found on 60 per cent of kale samples, was Dacthal/DCPA.
'EWG's 2019 Shopper's Guide to Pesticides in Produce™', Environmental Working Group, 20 March 2019.

P. 96. Cereals are not the most heavily fertilised food crops, but they cover more than half of the world's harvested area.
'Feeding the World', Food and Agricultural Organization of the United Nations, *FAO Statistical Yearbook 2013: world food and agriculture*, 2013, pp. 123–200.

P. 96. Of all the cereals, corn, wheat and rice use the most fertilisers … Oats, sorghum and millet have lower fertiliser needs.
Fertilizer use by crop', Food and Agricultural Organization of the United Nations, *FAO Fertilizer and Plant Nutrition Bulletin*, 17, 2006.

P. 96. More than half of the world's calories are provided by just three crops: rice, maize and wheat.
'Staple foods: what do people eat?', Food and Agriculture Organization of the United Nations, 1995.

P. 97. Oil palm trees produce more oil from less land than any other oil crop.

Sheil, D, Casson, A, et al, 'The impacts and opportunities of palm oil in Southeast Asia: what do we know and what do we need to know?', *CIFOR Occasional Paper*, 51, 2009.

P. 97. In 2019–2020, 75 million tonnes (165 billion pounds) of palm oil were produced worldwide, with 84 per cent coming from Indonesia and Malaysia.
United States Department of Agriculture Foreign Agricultural Service – Production, Supply and Distribution custom query.

P. 97. Oil palms take up around 10 per cent of the world's permanent crop land.
Sheil, D, Casson, A, et al, 'The impacts and opportunities of palm oil in Southeast Asia: what do we know and what do we need to know?', *CIFOR Occasional Paper*, 51, 2009.

P. 98. Palm oil is the sixth most heavily chemically fertilised crop in the world.
'Fertilizer use by crop', Food and Agricultural Organization of the United Nations, *FAO Fertilizer and Plant Nutrition Bulletin*, 17, 2006.

P. 98. The UN suggests peatland fires contribute around 5 per cent of human-caused carbon emissions.
Joosten, H, *The Global peatland CO_2 picture: peatland status and emissions in all countries of the world*, Wetlands International, 2009.

P. 98. The Roundtable on Sustainable Palm Oil (RSPO) now has over 4000 members worldwide.
'About', Roundtable on Sustainable Palm Oil, 2019.

P. 98. The RSPO currently certify about 20 per cent of global palm oil production.
Thomas, M, Buchanan, J, et al, 'Sustainable sourcing guide for palm oil users: a practical handbook for US consumer goods and retail companies', Conservation International and the World Wide Fund for Nature, May 2015.

P. 98. Many consider the [RSPO certified sustainable palm oil] standards to be weak and enforcement limited.
Morgans, CL, Meijaard, E, et al. 'Evaluating the effectiveness of palm oil certification in delivering multiple sustainability objectives ', *Environmental Research Letters*, 13(6), 12 June 2018.

P. 99. The US FDA requires that oils be declared by their common or usual name in food products.
'CFR – Code of Federal Regulations Title 21', US Food & Drug Administration, 1 April 2019.

P. 100. It is estimated that 70–90 per cent of the world's soybean crop is used as animal feed.
Eating up the Amazon, Greenpeace, April 2006.

P. 106. It's been estimated that the average Australian household throws away 20–25 per cent of everything they buy.
Food waste avoidance benchmark study 2009, NSW Environmental Protection Agency, September 2012.

P. 109. 10 per cent of the 88 million tonnes (194 billion pounds) of food waste created in the EU is linked to date marking.
Lyndhurst, B, and Directorate-General for Health and Food Safety (European Commission), 'Market study on date marking and other information provided on food labels and food waste prevention', EU Publications, 7 February 2018.

P. 133. In Australia, 87 per cent of food waste currently goes to landfill.
Pickin, J, Randell, P et al. *National waste report 2018*, Blue Environment Pty Ltd, 19 November 2018.

P. 133. Landfills are the third-largest source of human-related methane emissions in the US, accounting for more than 14 per cent of emissions.
'Basic information about landfill gas', United States Environmental Protection Agency, 2019.

P. 146. The Harvard Healthy Eating Plate was developed to address what the creators saw as deficiencies in government-produced healthy eating guidelines, which mix science with the influence of powerful agricultural interests.
Datz, T, 'Harvard serves up its own "Plate"', *The Harvard Gazette*, 14 September 2011.

index

Published in 2020 by Hardie Grant Books,
an imprint of Hardie Grant Publishing

Hardie Grant Books (Melbourne)
Building 1, 658 Church Street
Richmond, Victoria 3121

Hardie Grant Books (London)
5th & 6th Floors
52–54 Southwark Street
London SE1 1UN

hardiegrantbooks.com

A catalogue record for this
book is available from the
National Library of Australia

NATIONAL LIBRARY OF AUSTRALIA

The Less Waste No Fuss Kitchen
ISBN 978 1 74379 583 5

10 9 8 7 6 5 4 3 2 1

Publisher: Arwen Summers
Project Editor: Emily Hart
Editor: Sonja Heijn
Design Manager: Jessica Lowe
Designer: Vanessa Masci
Production Manager: Todd Rechner
Production Coordinator: Mietta Yans

Colour reproduction by Splitting Image
Colour Studio

Printed in China by Leo Paper Products LTD.

The Less Waste No Fuss Kitchen is a
low-waste project, with the editorial
and design processes performed
electronically. The book is printed on
stock certified by the Forest Stewardship
Council (FSC): the highest standard forest
certification scheme and a member of
ISEAL Alliance, the global association
for sustainability standards. The paper
is cut to size prior to printing to reduce
wastage, and any excess paper, plastic,
wood and metal (such as printing plates)
produced during the printing process
is recycled. The book is also printed
using sustainable soy-based inks, which
produce less volatile organic compounds
(VOCs) than petroleum-based
alternatives and make it easier for any
extra inventory to eventually be recycled.